PSYCHOLOGICAL ISSUES

VOL. IX, No. 1   MONOGRAPH 33

A CONSIDERATION OF SOME LEARNING VARIABLES IN THE CONTEXT OF PSYCHOANALYTIC THEORY:

TOWARD A PSYCHOANALYTIC LEARNING PERSPECTIVE

by

STANLEY I. GREENSPAN

INTERNATIONAL UNIVERSITIES PRESS, INC.
239 Park Avenue South   •   New York, N.Y. 10003

Library of Congress Catalog Card Number: 74-19890
ISBN: 0-8236-1050-0

Manufactured in the United States of America

PSYCHOLOGICAL ISSUES

Subscription per Volume, $25.00
Single Copies of This Number, $6.50

CONTENTS

ACKNOWLEDGMENTS

This monograph evolved from experiences over the course of a number of years, involving contact with many people who facilitated my education and growth and to whom I feel deeply grateful:

The faculty of the Yale University School of Medicine for their flexible, innovative program of medical education which stimulated questioning and original research.

At the Columbia Presbyterian Medical Center, Psychiatric Institute, Department of Psychiatry, Dr. Lawrence Kolb and Dr. Shervert Frazier and the many excellent teachers and supervisors for creating an educational program in psychiatry which provided basic clinical training and grounding in psychoanalytic theory as well as stimulation to question and seek out new areas of discovery. I would particularly like to thank Dr. Howard Hunt, Director of Psychological Research, who taught me a great deal about learning theory, which provided impetus for many of the ideas in this monograph. I would like also to thank Dr. Kenneth Greenspan for his valuable discussions and Ms. Helen Hans for her useful critiques.

At Hillcrest Children's Center, George Washington University Medical School, Dr. Reginald Lourie, Dr. Joseph Noshpitz, Dr. Nicolous Long, and Dr. Lawrence Cove for creating an educational program in child psychiatry which broadened my perspective and interest in early child development and further stimulated my interest in research.

The faculty of the Washington Psychoanalytic Institute for providing a rich psychoanalytic educational program which stresses both basic theory and technique and an appreciation of areas where further growth is indicated. Dr. Daniel Jaffe provided a useful critique of an earlier version of this manuscript.

At the National Institute of Mental Health, Laboratory of Psychology, I owe a special debt of gratitude to Dr. Morris Parloff for his encouragement and guidance, and for his extremely valuable discussions of and suggestions for the preliminary manuscripts. I am grateful, too, to Dr. Donald Burnham, also at NIMH, for patiently facilitating the clarification of difficult concepts, and to Dr. David Rosenthal for his general support of this research.

At the Mental Health Study Center, NIMH, Dr. Beryce MacLennan for her support of this project, and Dr. Milton Shore for his valuable discussion of the ideas contained in this monograph.

In addition, Ms. Mary Tarasco has my gratitude for her valuable contributions of theoretical and practical aspects of learning theory.

Dr. Herbert Schlesinger, Editor of *Psychological Issues,* has been extremely helpful in proposing suggestions for expansion and revision of this monograph.

It would be difficult to express enough appreciation to Marcie Giberman for her careful, understanding, and perceptive editorial help. A special thanks to Ms. Lillian Oksner and Ms. Ruth Bell for their careful typing and additional editorial help, and to Suzette H. Annin for her final editorial review.

And finally, I would like to express my special gratitude to the National Institute of Mental Health for its support of this work.

INTRODUCTION

Psychoanalysis conceptualizes the multiple determinants of behavior through a developmental and organizational consideration of the relationships between drives, inner structures, and the environment. A better understanding of the relative roles of these forces and how they interact might serve to expand accepted psychoanalytic theory (Holt, 1967). Any expansion of psychoanalytic theory must, however, be consistent with the parent body of thought.

One area which calls for further study is learning, in large part because current learning models do not meet the criterion of consistency and therefore remain outside the analytic framework. Rapaport (1959, p. 35) pointed out that although Hartmann's concept of automatization and Lewin's (1926) concept of ossification seemed to open up a new approach, the problem of learning has not yet been solved by psychoanalysis.

Particular learning variables have the potential to expand analytic understanding of how certain objective aspects of reality—external stimuli—operate as determinants of behavior. The problem is to make these variables acceptable to psychoanalysis in order that their potential be fully realized.

In this monograph I will attempt to find a solution to that problem. I will examine the psychoanalytic concept of reality and identify those areas that might be further expanded. A rationale for selecting certain learning variables will be provided in a brief discussion of learning theory. The conditions necessary for these variables to be acceptable to psychoanalytic theory will be stated. The dynamic, structural, economic, genetic, and adaptive viewpoints of psychoanalysis will be defined, and the learning variables examined in relation to each. It will be shown that the establishment of these relationships leads to a learning model which meets the conditions of acceptability.

The incorporation of the learning variables into the psychoanalytic framework will better enable us to understand aspects of the environment's effect on the formation of a structure and the behaviors which emerge from it. We can then consider the questions Rapaport (1959, p. 35) raised about how processes become structures, and those Hartmann, Kris, and Loewenstein (1946, pp. 37-38) raised about the optimum levels of frustration and gratification conducive to internalization. We can also consider questions about the environment's role in determining the specificity of behavior—that is, how behaviors are shaped from the ego's general tendency to respond—as well as its role in altering drive-related behaviors or making them resistant to change.

1

ASPECTS OF THE ENVIRONMENT THAT NEED FURTHER CLARIFICATION

A. The Role of Reality in Psychoanalytic Theory

In this section I will draw heavily on Rapaport's (1959, pp. 57-61) discussion of the role of reality in psychoanalytic psychology. According to him, reality in psychoanalytic theory designates the external sources of stimuli—including the subject's own body—but excepts the somatic sources of drives and affects. In this theory, external reality is the antithesis of psychological reality.

Freud's (1894) first concept of reality was that it was the target of defenses. His second concept of reality (Freud, 1900), which dominated psychoanalytic theory from 1900 to 1923, had two important aspects: the drive object and the secondary process. In this concept, external stimuli were accorded little significance in determining behavior. At the same time, however, certain elements of external stimuli—drive objects—were conceived as the precondition for drive discharge. Thus the effectiveness of the drives as the ultimate determinants of behavior was in part dependent on the availability of a drive object. In addition, Freud considered that the configurations of reality which prohibited drive actions were represented intrapsychically by the censorship. This, then, was a drive-centered conception of reality.

Rapaport observed that while early psychoanalytic theory may at times have given the impression that the organism is totally autonomous from its environment, Freud was never so blind as to take this extreme stand. But he did raise the question of the organism's relative autonomy from the environment.

The other aspect of Freud's second concept of reality, the secondary process, he asserted to reflect reality "truly," not merely in terms of how the drive object is to be reached, but in terms of real relationships between objects.

Freud's third concept of reality was forecast in his formulations of the two principles in mental functioning (1911), particularly the reality principle and reality testing. Whereas in his first concept defense was directed against reality and the memory of real events, and in his second concept defense was directed against the drive, in this third concept reality and drive appeared to be given relatively equal status. According to Freud, the ultimate motivation for defense is real danger. The drive is defended against, because if it were acted upon it would lead to a dangerous real situation. Thus defenses against drives came to represent reality, and their constituents came to have ego and superego structure; they became internalized regulators of behavior. In this concept, the focus on identification with objects of social reality implies that reality has not only a defensive, conflictual role but also an ego structure-forming role. The ego is conceived as a cohesive organization with a synthetic function of its own: to reconcile the demands of the id and the superego with reality (Freud, 1923). In this concept, reality shapes not only the ego but even the drives, which had previously been seen as unchanging.

The fourth concept of reality, which centers on Hartmann's (1939) contributions, Rapaport considered to be a radical development. Here the organism is a product of evolution and has already adapted, or is potentially adapted, to reality. The ego is the instrument of primary autonomy and guarantees man's "preparedness for an average expectable environment." The potential for the internalized regulation of behavior actualizes in the course of development of the ego, and thus the ego becomes man's vehicle for adaptation. In this model, reality and adaptiveness are the matrix of all behavior. Hartmann's concepts of relative autonomy, secondary autonomy, automatization, and neutralization provide a framework for understanding the development of the function of the secondary process as one of man's major adaptive means. Rapaport said, however, that even this schema seems to retain an essential duality of psychological and external reality.

Erikson (1956) goes beyond this theory and sees man as pre-adapted to not one average expectable environment but a whole evolving series of such environments, which he views as social rather than objective. Man's developing modes are selected and harnessed by the environment. Even here, however, Rapaport (1959, p. 61) argued that the concept of an objective reality disappears, and the major time and space coordinates of reality are subjective in the sense that they are relative to the individual and his society.

In this summary, the role of reality has been shown to have been expanded in psychoanalytic theory in a progression of steps. First it was a target of defense and provider of the drive object. Then it became a regulator of drive-determined behaviors and a vital component in the shaping of drives as well as in the formation of structures. Finally, it was seen to have an influence in shaping the organism's psychological system, as in Hartmann's conception of an average expectable environment to which the organism is potentially adapted, or in Erikson's conception of the social environment's meeting maturation and development halfway.

The psychoanalytic concept of reality has potential for even further expansion. Its present role as a determinant of behavior is seen mainly as it affects either the total psychological system or particular aspects of it. Alterations in the psychological system lead to alterations in behavior. Rapaport (1959, p. 61) said that even for Hartmann and Erikson, the essential duality of psychological and external reality is retained.

Models which focus on objective aspects of external reality can provide an additional perspective for psychoanalysis. These aspects of reality influence behavior independent of their subjective representation.

Because psychoanalysis is predominantly a representational psychology, it may be difficult for its adherents to accept the idea that aspects of reality may influence behavior independent of their psychic representation. External events are usually thought to exert their influence on behavior through their conscious and unconscious meanings. Objective properties of stimuli which may act independently of their subjective meanings are often thought to have meanings or representational elements which go unrecognized. It is not uncommon for the sensitive analyst to amaze students at a case conference by pointing out the possible unrecognized meanings of certain events in a patient's life.

While all external events may have some representational properties, the question remains, do certain aspects of these events exert an influence which is independent of representation? To explore this question operationally, the possibility that meanings exist for every event may be accepted. However, it would be important to determine what the implications of these meanings are for behavior. To explore this, the following propositions could be formulated. If a particular event exerts its influence on a person through its meanings, then the influence of that event should be unique to that person because of the particular meanings that his life experience will have fostered. If an event exerts its influence independent of its meanings, then the unique properties of the event rather than the life experiences of the person should determine its influence. If the first proposition is true, a constant external event would have at least somewhat different implications for different persons, since each would endow it with different meanings. But if the second proposition is true, a constant external event would have the same implications for different persons.

These two propositions and the predictions derived from them make it possible to view external phenomena operationally in terms of how an external event exerts its influence, directly through its objective properties, or through its subjective meanings or representations. This approach avoids the semantic struggle over whether every event has a conscious or unconscious representation, and instead focuses attention on the more important issue: which properties of a complex external stimulus configuration have implications for which aspects of behavior. A particular aspect of a behavior may be influenced by an external stimulus configuration in two ways—through the representation or meaning of the stimulus, and directly through certain properties of the stimulus. The test for the latter possibility is clear: vary the human subjects, or even the species, but maintain a constant stimulus and determine if certain aspects of behavior remain constant. The components of the behavior which remain constant will be directly dependent on a property of the stimulus. If a subjective representation of this component of the behavior exists, it will be a parallel rather than a directly or intermediarily determining phenomenon.

There are models which conceptualize the relationships between stimuli and responses which operate independently of subjective representations. Within these models it is possible to observe the direct functional relationships between aspects of a stimulus and aspects of behavior. For example, as will be described in some detail below, the pattern with which a behavior is rewarded may have a direct influence on aspects of that behavior, such as its resistance to change, which will hold for different persons as well as for some different species.

However, the objective properties of a stimulus do not exert their influence in a pure culture. Later on, the more complex interrelationships between the psychoanalytic representational system as conceptualized by the metapsychological points of view and objective properties of stimuli will be described.

Models which focus on objective properties of external stimuli have been developed within academic psychology, in which studies of stimulus-controlled behavior have shown that external stimuli may act as direct determinants of behavior. These models will be considered in the next section.

B. Learning Theories

I will not attempt to review all the many different theories of learning, but will focus on operant learning, the approach which seems to offer the most for the development of a psychoanalytic learning perspective. I have chosen this approach because it identifies certain variables that exert a direct determining effect on behavior. These variables are objective and complement the variables considered by psychoanalytic theory.

To understand why the operant learning approach has been selected, a brief general discussion of learning will be useful. For purposes of simplification, learning theories can be divided into those that rest upon hypothesized internal constructs and conceptualize the processing of stimuli, and those that do not rest on hypothesized internal constructs and view behavior strictly in terms of observable environmental phenomena. Examples of the former are cognitive development theories; an example of the latter is operant conditioning theory.

In the processing model, stimuli impinge upon the organism, whereupon the organism processes these stimuli and then acts.

The processing of a stimulus involves its perception, its storage, its relationship with other stored stimuli, its organization, its reorganization, its role in the further development of the processing equipment, and finally its role in determining behavior. Obviously there can be many intermediate and complex steps in this processing. They all, however, contribute to an association between what goes into the organism and what comes out.

Psychoanalysis belongs among the approaches that study the processing of stimuli. It is unique, however, in that it studies the processing of drives—those special stimuli which arise from within the organism. In the psychoanalytic model, these inner stimuli interact with outer stimuli. Both contribute to the processing equipment, and both lead to behavioral output. In addition, biological maturational factors also influence the drives and the processing equipment.

Other processing models do not account for the influence of the drives. They tend to view the processing under constant drive conditions. Wolff (1960) has said that Piaget did not study the state of the organism. Yet the processing models are more similar than dissimilar. The interface between the vicissitudes of the drives and certain aspects of ego functioning may be further clarified through additional observation and experimentation.

Models which attempt to explain the processing of stimuli may be seen as focusing on subjective reality in the sense that Rapaport considered psychoanalytic ego psychology to maintain the duality between subjective and objective reality. The processing equipment evolves from the interaction of the person's maturational processes with his environment. The structure of that equipment is a determinant of how the person experiences his world.

C. OPERANT LEARNING THEORY—OBJECTIVE PROPERTIES OF STIMULI

Further to explore the role of reality requires that we first ask whether external stimuli have a role other than in relation to the drives and the processing equipment. If so, do these independent properties also influence behavior? Stated another way, can models which ignore the structure of the internal equipment—and in that sense, internal experience itself—and instead focus on direct functional relationships between properties of external events and behavior be both relevant and useful to psychoanalysis? The answer is yes, and will be amplified in the following sections.

A model which focuses on the objective properties of stimuli as determinants of behavior is operant learning theory (Skinner, 1938). The objective aspects of reality are the spatial and temporal qualities of stimuli: size, shape, color, intensity, and other objective properties. Stimuli also have temporal relationships with behaviors. A stimulus may occur before a behavior, after a behavior, together with a behavior, or independently of a behavior. If a stimulus occurs in relation to a behavior, it may occur in many differing schedules. For example, a stimulus which occurs after a behavior and is a consequence of that behavior may occur each time the behavior is emitted, or it may follow the behavior only under certain conditions—say, every fifth time the behavior is emitted.

These properties of stimuli are of a different dimension than those currently embraced by psychoanalytic theory. They exert an influence on behavior that is independent of the meaning they may have for the behaving person. In this sense they are objective rather than subjective. In most situations, for example, praise from one's superior is perceived as a reward. For some persons, however—for example, those with prominent masochistic tendencies—praise may not be thus perceived. Whether or not an outer stimulus is experienced as rewarding depends on the individual's personality organization. Reality in this sense is subjective. Once the stimulus becomes rewarding, however, it can then be presented in many different schedules and can be contingent on different behaviors, regardless of the individual's personality organization. For example, if the schedule of rewards is a variable ratio schedule, the rate of emission of the behavior contingent upon it will be higher than if the schedule is a fixed interval schedule. In the case of a variable interval schedule, the number of responses that will occur without reinforcement before responding declines will be greater than if the schedule is a continuous one.[1] Once the stimulus is established as reinforcing, and a particular behavior becomes contingent upon it, the effects of

[1]In a variable ratio schedule, behavior is reinforced only after a certain number of responses are emitted. The number changes from reinforcement to reinforcement. In an interval schedule, behavior is reinforced after certain time periods have elapsed. In a fixed interval schedule, the time periods are constant. In a variable interval schedule, the time periods change. In a continuous schedule, each response is reinforced (Ferster and Skinner, 1957).

these schedules can be experimentally reproduced. They can be shown to have valid relationships to behavior that are independent of the person's personality organization. These properties of the stimulus are therefore objective in the sense that Rapaport (1959, p. 61) held psychoanalytic theory to maintain the duality between subjective and objective reality. The implications of these objective properties of stimuli will be considered later on.

Operant learning theory is an interactional model which provides for a conceptualization of the environmental variables preceding and following certain responses. For those unfamiliar with it, an introduction to its concepts follows.

1. OPERANT LEARNING CONCEPTS

"In operant learning, we think of behavior as segmented into units called *responses*. We think of the environment as segmented into units called *stimuli*. Unfortunately, both terms are somewhat misleading, because they do not refer in operant conditioning to what their ordinary meanings suggest. Responses, the units of behavior, need not be 'replies' to the environment.... Nor do stimuli necessarily incite the organism to action" (Reynolds, 1968, p. 6).[2]

Operants are emitted responses or behaviors. The frequency of occurrence of an operant is influenced by its consequences—that is, by the environmental event that follows it. If a stimulus, in consequence of a response, increases the probability that a response will recur in the future, the stimulus is called a *positive reinforcer*. If a stimulus removal, in consequence of a response, increases the probability that a response will recur in the future, the stimulus is called an aversive stimulus or *negative reinforcer*. To simplify this discussion, I will limit it to positive reinforcers.

Stimuli such as food and water, which reinforce behavior without the organism's having had previous experience with them, are "primary" or unconditioned reinforcers. Other stimuli, which ac-

---

[2]The responses composing behavior may be separated into two classes called *operants* and *respondents*. Respondents are influenced by the stimuli which precede them, eliciting stimuli. These stimuli elicit relatively fixed and stereotyped responses, the respondents mentioned above. Respondent or classical or Pavlovian conditioning will be considered later. In contrast to respondents, which are influenced by the stimuli which precede them, operants are emitted behavior which are influenced by their consequences, the stimuli which follow them. For a more complete introductory discussion of operant theory than is possible here, consult *A Primer of Operant Conditioning*, by G. S. Reynolds (1968).

quire the power to reinforce operants owing to the organism's experiences—that is, by being paired with primary reinforcers—are "secondary" or conditioned reinforcers.

Most operants occur with high frequency only under certain conditions. For example, an animal may be trained to press a lever only when a light goes on. The stimuli which control the operant response by being the occasion for it are called *discriminative stimuli.*

An operant will occur with high frequency in the presence of discriminative stimuli which have accompanied it in the past and set the occasion for its reinforcement.

Other aspects of the operant paradigm also deserve attention. The organism has a relative discriminatory capacity which may determine whether or not it can distinguish between two stimuli. For example, infants cannot discriminate among various geometric shapes as well as adults can. By and large, the younger the organism, the poorer its discriminatory capacity. It will tend to respond to similar stimuli in a similar manner; that is, it will tend to generalize stimuli. The discriminatory capacity of the organism also influences its ability to discriminate among conditioned reinforcers. Thus an infant, more than an adult, will tend to generalize among conditioned reinforcers.

Responses can also become generalized. Reinforcement of an operant increases not only the frequency of that operant but of some similar responses. After reinforcement of the response *dada,* for example, a baby would be likely soon to say *ba-ba* and *ga-ga.* Learning and innate capacities at various ages determine the degree to which finer and finer responses can be singled out. Here also a baby tends to generalize more than an adult.

As opposed to response or discriminative stimulus generalization, under certain conditions the phenomenon of behavioral contrast will occur. Behavioral contrast may occur when a behavior is under the control of a number of discriminative stimuli. If reinforcement ceases in the presence of one discriminative stimulus (an extinction procedure) the behavior may eventually decrease in the presence of that stimulus. However, at the same time it may increase in the presence of the other discriminative stimuli with no change in the schedule of reinforcement. For example, a child who can discriminate between school and home may behave aggressively in both. If his aggressive behavior is systematically not reinforced in school and therefore extinguished there, it may increase at home even though there are no changes in the latter. Instead of the results from school generalizing, behavioral contrast occurs.

Another characteristic of the organism is its response to deprivation, that is, limiting its exposure to a particular positive reinforcer. A deprivation operation can multiply the effects of this reinforcer. A baby who was fed each time he cried will be more likely to cry with greater frequency if food is subsequently withheld. Such deprivation can increase many behaviors, some of which are not directly associated with obtaining the withheld reinforcer.

Some additional processes which will be referred to later are those of differential reinforcement and shaping. Differential reinforcement refers to the selective reinforcement of one behavior and the selective nonreinforcement of another. It may also refer to the selective reinforcement of a behavior under one set of conditions (discriminative stimuli) and selective nonreinforcement of a behavior under another set of conditions. Through this process certain behaviors can be selected and increased in frequency, while others are made to recede and decrease in frequency. Also through this process, discriminative learning may occur. If an organism is reinforced for a behavior in one condition (red light) but not in another (blue light), it may learn to discriminate between the different conditions, and to respond only in the condition which produces reinforcement.

Shaping refers to the learning of new behavior through a series of steps. To teach a pigeon to press a lever, first any activity may be reinforced. Then any movement toward the lever is differentially reinforced. Then further movement toward the lever is selectively reinforced. Then standing at the lever is differentially reinforced. Following this, any capricious movement toward the lever is differentially reinforced. Finally, a capricious pressing of the lever will be reinforced. Shaping refers to this gradual process of establishing one behavior followed by differentially reinforcing another toward an ultimate goal behavior. The skill of the shaper is significant in selecting the most effective steps. The organization of the series of steps is referred to as a *program*—as in *programmed* learning.

The schedule of reinforcement is another important parameter.

Varying the schedule of reinforcement influences the frequency with which an operant is emitted, and the time interval, pattern, and number of responses that will occur without reinforcement before the frequency of the operant is significantly reduced (the extinction pattern). Intermittent schedules, for example, can maintain operants without reinforcement for long periods of time. Examples of simple schedules of reinforcement follow:

Continuous Schedules. Each response is reinforced.

Ratio Schedules. A certain number of responses must be emitted before one response is reinforced.

Interval Schedules. A given interval of time must elapse before a response can be reinforced.

Variable and Fixed Schedules. Ratio or interval schedules may be either variable or fixed. When a variable ratio or interval schedule is operant, the number of responses or time intervals required for one reinforcement varies from reinforcement to reinforcement in a repeating fashion (10 responses required, then 15 responses required, then 13 responses required; or 10 seconds, 9 seconds, 8 seconds, etc.). When a fixed ratio or interval schedule is operant, the number of responses or the time period required for one reinforcement is fixed (10 responses, 10 responses, or 10 seconds, 10 seconds, etc.).

Multiple Schedules. Two or more independent schedules may be presented successively, each in the presence of its own discriminative stimulus.

Compound, Conjunctive, Alternative, Interlocking, and Concurrent Schedules. These are other complex schedules, which will not be discussed here. Each schedule has its own implications for the behavior it is influencing. For a detailed review, see Ferster and Skinner (1957). A brief review of some of their findings is appropriate here.

Each schedule affects the extinction time of a behavior, the pattern of this extinction, and aspects of the pattern of this behavior during its maintenance.

Extinction refers to what occurs to a behavior after reinforcement ceases. The extinction time refers to the amount of time between the cessation of reinforcement and the drop of response to a constant low level. Each schedule affects the extinction time differently. For example, behavior which is influenced by interval schedules, such as a variable interval schedule with long intervals, decreases in frequency rather slowly; a continuous schedule causes behavior to decrease in frequency more rapidly.

Behaviors under the control of interval schedules, particularly those with long intervals between reinforcements, will undergo longer extinction time and will therefore be more resistant to change than behaviors under the control of relatively continuous schedules.

The pattern of extinction refers to the pattern of the behavior as it undergoes extinction. For example, behavior under the control of a fixed interval schedule will undergo extinction by bursts of alternate decline and acceleration of response. Shortly after the time when reinforcement would have occurred, response ceases abruptly. This is followed by an acceleration of response and another abrupt decline, and so on, until a constant low rate of response is reached. For a variable ratio schedule, a sustained high response rate may be emitted during extinction, with increasingly longer periods of no response until full extinction is reached. A variable interval schedule leads to a slow, steady extinction pattern; responses decrease in frequency evenly and slowly. The pattern of extinction may have interesting implications for characterizing different patterns of response to frustration or nonreinforcement.

The schedule of reinforcement also has implications for aspects of behavior during maintenance of response. Some schedules, for example, a variable ratio schedule, maintain behavior at high rates; others, for example, a variable interval schedule, maintain behavior at low rates. Some schedules lead to continuous response, others lead to intermittent response. The implications of characteristics of behavior which are determined by their schedule of reinforcement will be considered later.

Operant learning theory should not be confused with classical or respondent conditioning. Classical learning theory is not an interactional learning theory. The stimulus-response patterns central to its concepts, however, do come under operant control. According to classical theory, an unconditioned stimulus leads to an automatic, often physiological, response, such as a dog's salivating at the sight of food. Stimuli paired with the original unconditioned stimulus can elicit the same response. Hence, with repeated conditioning, a bell can become the stimulus for eliciting a salivating response. This model has been adopted by some to explain in part various clinical states such as phobias. It has also been presented as part of the explanation for certain behavioral therapies employing counterconditioning techniques. It should be made clear, however, that no matter what elicits a response, if this response is followed by a stimulus which is a consequence of the response, the stimulus can become a reinforcer and also have control over the response. The response is therefore under operant control. It is possible to conceptualize the automatic or conditioned stimulus-response pattern as a complex response class ($R_{(S-R)}$), in which the response class is defined by the stimulus and the response. For example, we could label the response class "salivating in response to food," or "salivating in response to a bell," or "avoiding threatening situations," as in the case of phobias, or "feeling anxiety upon seeing a snake." Through this sort of conceptualization, it is possible to use a traditional operant learning theory analysis of the interactional variables, in which there is a discriminative stimulus, a response, and a reinforcing stimulus (Ds-(R)-Rs), to include classical conditioned learning. The definition of the response class (that is, $R_{(S-R)}$) takes into account the classical conditioned learning.

Consider the patient who has functional abdominal pain whenever he comes into close contact with a woman. A classical learning analysis might lead to the hypothesis that the proximity of a woman is a conditioned stimulus (S^c) which elicits the response (R) abdominal pain. It might be postulated that at one point in his early life this patient was frightened by an unconditioned stimulus (S^u) (e.g., potential physical injury), and that part of his automatic fear response was abdominal pain. It could then be further postulated that later in his development the stimulus configuration represented by proximity to a woman became paired with the original unconditioned stimulus and thereby became a conditioned stimulus which elicited abdominal pain. The situation is therefore $S^c \to R$, in which the stimulus precedes and elicits the response. The conditioned stimulus, therefore, controls the response. Assume that this patient is in a hospital, and most of the time when he has abdominal pain his doctor quickly comes to see him. Further assume that he experiences these visits by his doctor as highly gratifying. These visits by his doctor can therefore be conceptualized as providing reinforcement. Because the doctor's visits are a consequence of the abdominal pain, the pain response increases in frequency and is under the control of this reinforcement. The sight of the doctor makes it possible for reinforcement to occur (only when the doctor is in the hospital are visits from him possible). Thus, the sight of the doctor can come to operate as a discriminative stimulus; it sets the occasion for reinforcement. Therefore, upon seeing his doctor, the patient may experience abdominal pain because in the past the pain has had as its consequence a visit from the doctor. The experience of the pain is as real as it was when the proximity of a woman stimulated it; only in this situation it is under operant control. Whereas initially the stimulus which controlled the abdominal pain preceded it as a conditioned stimulus (S^c), now the stimulus which influences the response occurs as a consequence of the response. The abdominal pain response which was initially part of a conditioned response pattern can, by this sequence of events, become the response in the operant paradigm (Ds-(R)-Rs). Now either the sight of the doctor sets the occasion for the pain because the doctor's visits have been a consequence of the pain, or the proximity of a woman elicits the pain because women are the conditioned stimulus for this response.

A classical learning therapist might use a counterconditioning technique to break the $S^c \rightarrow R$ link. The patient might first be taught deep relaxation and then instructed to relax while he is exposed to a series of graded stimulus configurations, at first pictures of women, then ultimately perhaps a real woman. The relaxation would be incompatible with the abdominal pain and the link would be broken.

An operant learning therapist would seek out the reinforcers maintaining the abdominal pain. He might then attempt to arrange the patient's environment so that reinforcement of the pain responses would be replaced by systematic reinforcement of responses incompatible with pain, such as a feeling of well-being.

Behavioral therapies often make use of both kinds of learning, and a combined model is necessary to understand how they work. I will not discuss this model here. It should be noted, however, that the school of classical learning does not study environmental interactional variables. Rather, it studies learned stimulus-response relationships as a function of automatic or unconditioned S-R patterns. Operant learning, which can incorporate classical learning, is, I believe, the proper counterpoint for psychoanalytic theory.

2. AN EXAMPLE

Operant learning focuses on aspects of the environment's role in the selection, maintenance, and modification of behavior. To illustrate the relationship between variables focused on by operant learning and psychodynamic approaches, let us analyze the relatively simple behavior of a particular infant. Later it will be apparent that this same analysis can be applied to complex behavior.

The baby is banging his head on his crib. Upon consultation, a pediatrician concludes that the infant's head-banging is due to maternal deprivation. The mother is told of her infant's need for love and nurturance and is instructed to hold her baby more frequently and to give him more love and attention. The mother follows these instructions, but subsequently the baby's head-banging increases rather than decreases. On a second consultation, the physician learns that mother holds her baby only when she hears him banging his head. Since the mother's attention is obviously a consequence of the head-banging, he concludes that the infant is inadvertently being rewarded for it. The physician again points out to the mother the infant's need for more love and attention and urges that they work together to try to understand the problem. He. emphasizes, however, that it is important to stop the head-banging as soon as possible. He instructs the mother to pick up her baby at various times, not only when he is banging his head. The mother follows his instructions. Most of the time she does not respond to the head-banging. Occasionally, however, perhaps only every fifth to tenth time she hears a loud noise, she goes in to check on him and at those times holds him. But with this change, the head-banging increases even more, and both mother and physician are perplexed.

Reviewing this situation may enable us to isolate the variables involved. In response to an intense feeling of maternal deprivation, the infant displays chaotic behavior, such as kicking, crying, and head-banging. One aspect of the mother's depriving her infant was that she held him only as a consequence of his head-banging and was in this way selecting this behavior from the child's repertory.[3] A further look at the manner in which the deprivation occurred explains, in part at least, the increase in the baby's head-banging. In attempting to nurture her infant more appropriately, the mother ceased responding to almost every instance of head-banging. But by coming in to hold her baby at various times and every fifth to tenth time he banged his head, the mother changed the reinforcement schedule from a nearly continuous one to a complex intermittent one. Intermittent schedules of reinforcement have been found to increase the frequency of behaviors and to make them more resistant to change. (See Ferster and Skinner [1957] for discussion of the implications of different schedules of reinforcement for behavior.)

This simplified example illustrates that when there is maladaptive behavior, there is always interaction between the underlying cause of the behavior, the behavior itself, and the environmental events which may be influencing it, as shown in Figure 1.

a. *Psychodynamic Aspects.* Part 1 of Figure 1 represents a broad overview of the psychodynamic model of behavior. An organism's drives and mental apparatus, both regulated by certain general psychodynamic principles, form a dynamic network that results in behavior ("behavior" is used in a broad sense to include responses that are directed outward and those that are directed inward). This network and its impact on behavior are influenced by biological maturational factors as well as by environmental events.

According to this model, the environment influences behavior through its effect on this complex network. Recent advances in ego psychology have focused on the relationship between the ego and the environment. The adaptational point of view, the conceptions of the conflict-free sphere and relative autonomy, are concerned with how the environment affects the development or functioning of aspects of the mental apparatus. Yet another determinant of behavior can be clearly seen in our case.

---

[3]The process is not as simple as described here. The final behavior is most probably a result of gradual shaping through differential reinforcement. The infant may at first only rub his head on the crib. If the mother reinforces this behavior by picking him up each time he does so, rubbing will increase in frequency. But then the infant may rub particularly hard on one occasion. If the mother picks him up as a consequence of this hard rubbing, while having stopped picking him up as a consequence of less hard rubbing, hard rubbing will increase in frequency. If next the same sequence occurs when the infant bangs his head on the crib, then head-banging will increase in frequency. The nonreinforcement of the established response (rubbing) and the selective reinforcement of the next response (hard rubbing) is an illustration of differential reinforcement.

Part I—Psychodynamic Theory

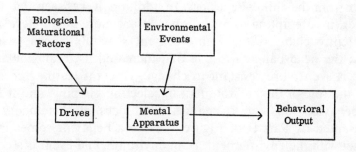

Part II—Operant Learning Theory

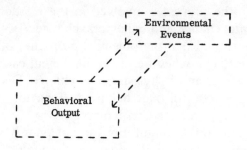

Part III—Combined Model

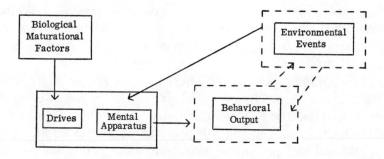

Figure 1. Solid arrows indicate processes conceptualized by psychodynamic theory; broken arrows indicate processes conceptualized by operant learning theory.

b. *Learning Aspects.* It has been suggested that a state of deprivation may lead either to general discharge or to lack of discharge. It has also been shown that the mother, in holding her baby as a consequence of his head-banging, had selected this particular behavior from the child's repertory. In addition, it was seen that the mother, in attempting to nurture her infant more adequately, inadvertently changed the reinforcement schedule which maintained the head-banging to one that increased its frequency and made it even more resistant to change. Operant learning recognizes the role of the environment in selecting, shaping, and making behavior resistant to change. The focus of this theory is represented by Part II of Figure 1. Here a behavior comes into contact with the environment. If an environmental event is a consequence of this behavior, it works back on the behavior to modify it in form, frequency, or resistance to change. Fundamental to operant learning are the processes involved in the relationships between environmental change and behavioral change.

It has been demonstrated that the objective properties of stimuli can affect behavior. The schedule of reinforcement can affect the frequency of behavior and its resistance to change. Discriminative stimuli can exert control over behavior. Behavior can be altered, or new behavior introduced, with a program.

The laws relating stimulus configurations to behavior have become more complex than the example indicates. Students of operant learning theory have expanded their conceptions to include the conditions which affect the efficacy of stimuli and antecedent stimulus configurations (Goldiamond, 1968; see also Weiner, 1964, 1965; and Gewirtz, 1969). For this discussion, however, it is important only to demonstrate that objective properties of stimuli have effects on behavior.

The additional perspective offered by an appreciation of the variables recognized by operant learning theory might easily be overlooked because of a "commonsense" or intuitive appreciation of their importance in general or lay terms. For example, in the hypothetical case presented, the schedule of reinforcement determined the frequency and resistance to change of the infant's head-banging. It could be postulated that inconsistent or unpredictable mothering explains these aspects of the head-banging. This explanation would certainly be valid. The concept of the reinforcement schedule allows us, however, to examine a specific dimension of what we mean by "inconsistent." How inconsistent? If we define the mother's attention as a reinforcer, we can classify the type of attention or inattention in terms of the type of reinforcement schedule. From our experimental data we can hypothesize about the implications of different kinds of inconsistency—that is, the schedule of reinforcement—for the frequency and resistance to change of particular behaviors. Certain schedules will lead to a high frequency of head-banging, whereas others will make it highly resistant to change. Of course, examining a specific dimension of inconsistency does not preclude paying attention to other aspects of inconsistent mothering such as the mother's ambivalence and the components of the quality of her care. What is being emphasized here is that an examination of a specific quantifiable dimension of experience can enhance our understanding of the multiple determinants of behavior.

Similarly, one could focus on the consistency of a mother's response to her infant. Generally, we believe that consistent mothering leads to healthy development. But how much consistency is optimal? We know that some frustration is necessary as well. Again, how much frustration is optimal? What are the implications of too little frustration or too much frustration for both the stability and the flexibility of the developing personality? In general terms, we know that too little frustration may hamper structure formation. What we do not have are ways of looking more closely at these ideas of too little or too much attention and frustration in terms of their significance for behavior. Here the reinforcement schedule, with its implications for the frequency, stability, and resistance to change of behavior, may provide a framework for answering some of these important questions.

It is known, for example, that behavior reinforced on a highly continuous schedule is easily and quickly extinguished; that is, the behavior is not stable. The implications of different schedules of reinforcement for behavioral extinction and for behavioral stability could lead to a fuller understanding of the conditions which foster too little structuralization, overstructuralization, certain defense styles, etc. These matters will be considered in more detail in a discussion of the implications of a psychoanalytic learning perspective.

D. The Antithesis between the Psychoanalytic and Learning Models

Bringing the concepts of operant learning theory into a psychoanalytic perspective is no simple matter. Operant learning theory grew out of the behavioral school of psychology which focused on what organisms *do* rather than on what they think and feel. The emphasis was on understanding observable behavior in terms of the stimuli which control it: stimulus-response relationships. Psychoanalytic theorists, on the other hand, while concerned with what people do, are more concerned with what they think and feel. Behavior is examined in terms of a complex, underlying psychic organization.

The two theories not only represent different interests but reflect a fundamental difference in assumptions about behavior. The behaviorist views behavior as a discrete entity under discrete stimulus control. As such, behavior is continually formed and continually open to modification by a change in the relevant environmental variables, the controlling stimuli. The psychodynamic theorist, however, often views behavior from various perspectives: dynamic, genetic, economic, structural, and adaptive. Behavioral change may not represent intrapsychic structural change, and intrapsychic structural change may not be observable in behavior. The psychoanalytic framework will be further discussed in the next chapter.

These disparate views of behavior and the therapeutic techniques which have derived from them—conditioning versus psychodynamic—have led to a marked schism between the two approaches. But there has also been some interest in bringing them closer together. Attempts at practical combinations of the techniques developed from the two theories have been made (Bandura, 1967; Cahoon, 1968; Marks and Gelder, 1966; Miller, 1964, 1969; Weitzman, 1967), as well as attempts at formulating various clinical states within the context of one and then the other (Akutawaga, 1968; Brady, 1967; see also Dollard and Miller, 1950; Marmor, 1969; Mowrer, 1950). A unifying model acceptable to both groups has been advocated (Hunt and Dyrud, 1968; Wolf, 1969; Woody, 1968).

The use of some psychodynamic principles in the context of behavior therapy technique has been described by Feather and Rhoads

(1972). Their suggestion is that behavioral interventions such as systematic desensitization may be directed at internal conflicts rather than at external stimuli. They do not, however, explore their approach systematically from the side of the psychoanalytic model, particularly with reference to current ego psychology.

The same criticism applies to an article by Birk and Brinkley-Birk (1974). They present a paradigm for using behavioral and psychoanalytic principles in a complementary manner to deal with the early learning that shapes behavior as well as the current behavior itself. The therapist, they suggest, can function as a transference figure to facilitate the understanding of early learning and at the same time can act as an instrument of numerous behavioral techniques (e.g., reinforcer/punisher, model, contingency arranger, etc.) to alter current behavior.

In their theory building, however, the authors refer only to Freud's topographical model (unconscious, preconscious, conscious) and ignore structural theory, object relations theory, and current ego psychology. A common shortcoming of these recent attempts at integrating psychoanalytic and behavioral learning models has been to consider only certain elements of psychoanalytic theory. This has led to a misrepresentation of psychoanalysis, theoretically inconsistent models, and oversimplified clinical techniques.

Another effort to bring the two models closer together focuses on the practical indications for using behavior modification in dynamically oriented clinical and educational settings (Blom, 1972). In a discussion of the wide variety of types of psychopathology, Marmor (1971) has also suggested bringing psychodynamic and behavioral techniques closer together, emphasizing that the processes of one are in fact operative in the therapeutic approaches of the other in any event. Noting that the processes of one are operative in the therapeutic approach of the other, however, is just the first step and in itself can be misleading.

One can examine complex clinical phenomena from many theoretical frames of reference. Advocates of opposing theories can easily claim that their model better explains and is more open to scientific study than the others.

A tempting, but often unproductive, tendency has been for each school to attempt to account for the other's major and specific findings with minor and general concepts of its own. For example, to think of reinforcement in terms of expectations obscures the contribution that reinforcement theorists have made to our understanding of how varying the schedule of reinforcement can alter the frequency of certain behaviors. Similarly, to account for the importance of the genetic approach in terms of the history of reinforcement obscures the wealth of observational and theoretical contributions psychoanalysis has made to understanding the specific relationship between early experiences and later personality patterns.

Insofar as a theory or model is an abstraction, it must be assessed in terms of its applicability to certain phenomena. What is necessary to maximize our understanding of behavior is a theoretical framework which allows the variables focused on by each discipline to be viewed in interaction. Let us examine the conditions of psychoanalytic theory that must be met for additional variables to be compatibly conceptualized within its framework.

2

CONDITIONS THAT NEED TO BE MET FOR A PSYCHOANALYTIC LEARNING THEORY

Two criteria must be met for a learning model to be an acceptable addition to psychoanalytic theory. One, it must provide a way of looking at a behavior which will reveal some new aspect or dimension of it. In psychoanalytic theory reality was first seen in terms of the drives, then in terms of structures (particularly the ego structure), and finally in terms of adaptation. Inclusion of the learning variables within the analytic framework would make it possible to study how aspects of stimuli which are independent of their subjective meanings can also act as determinants of behavior. Two, in order to be included within the analytic framework, the learning variables must be so conceptualized that they are functionally related to the established psychoanalytic points of view.

Rapaport (1959, pp. 65-72) maintained that usually no single determinant has the dominant role in behavior. He noted that in behavioral research, when favorable conditions make one determinant dominant, the investigator tends to conclude that he has confirmed the predicted functional relationship. Regrettably, the attempt to repeat the particular observation or experiment often fails, because in the replication either the same behavior appears even though a different determinant is dominant, or a different behavior appears even though the same determinant has remained dominant. This is a clear statement of the psychoanalytic concept of multiple determination.

Following this concept, psychoanalytic theory requires the exploration of all possible functional relationships among its variables. As Rapaport (1959) put it,

Not that each behavior is a microcosm which reflects the macrocosm of the personality but rather that an explanation of behavior, in order to have any claim to completeness, must specify its place in the functional and structural framework of the total personality and therefore must include statements about the degree and kind of involvement in the behavior in question of all the relevant conceptualized aspects of personality [p. 43].

To illustrate, he demonstrated how each of the major psychoanalytic perspectives can be treated as an independent, intervening, or dependent variable (pp. 65-72). While it is not necessary to this discussion to review his demonstration in detail, it is important to spell out what it means. The functional relationships among all the variables must be clear.

Rapaport (1959, pp. 65-72) held that stimulus-response psychology appears to be a limiting case of a high degree of autonomy or automatization. Only in situations in which certain intervening variables—thoughts or affects—are absent is there a direct relationship between a stimulus or motivation and a behavior. This criticism of operant learning theory has merit only if we accept operant learning theory as a complete explanation for the complex properties of a given behavioral phenomenon. It cannot be denied that this model, because of its focused method of investigation, has established certain laws which clarify aspects of particular functional relationships. If it becomes possible to define these relationships as another determinant of behavior in the same way psychoanalytic theory defines each of its perspectives as one of many determinants of behavior, the contributions of operant learning theory will provide an additional point of view. For this to be the case, the operant learning variables must be consistent with the organization of psychoanalytic theory.

For the operant learning model to apply to natural situations where there are multiple relationships between drives, defenses, structures, reality, and behavior, the functional relationships between the operant learning variables and each metapsychological perspective must be developed.

In the following discussion I will develop a learning perspective in the context of psychoanalytic theory. Both theories will be used to develop a model in which the learning variables are consistent with the psychoanalytic points of view. It will be shown how stimuli and the responses they influence can be defined by each meta-psychological viewpoint. The dynamic point of view will identify the relevant responses and the reinforcing and discriminative stimuli. The genetic point of view will define broad classes of stimuli and responses from a developmental perspective. The economic point of view will emphasize the efficacy and dominance of the stimulus classes, as well as the rigidity of the response classes. The structural point of view will further define the stimulus and response classes in terms of their broadness, their ingredients, and their relationships with each other. The adaptive point of view will demonstrate how classes of stimuli and responses can be defined, not only by drives and structures, but by the interaction of the ego with the environment. It will be shown how each metapsychological perspective can contribute to the definition of the learning variables, just as each of the analytic perspectives contributes to the definition of the others. The learning variables will be conceptualized within the psychoanalytic framework. It should be emphasized that while the major emphasis of the following discussions will be the development of a psychoanalytic learning point of view, this additional point of view is not intended to supersede or diminish the importance of any of the established points of view. On the contrary, the learning point of view will be a useful addition to psychoanalytic theory only to the degree that it is functionally related to the established analytic points of view and that it provides additional understanding of the multiple determination of behavior.

It should also be emphasized that the metapsychological points of view are a series of high-order abstractions which help us to understand and study the complexities of human personality functioning. To the extent that they are abstractions, the divisions between them are artificial. Behavioral phenomena may not always be so easily compartmentalized. However, with the acceptance of these limitations, such compartmentalization is useful to organize old observations and stimulate new ones. The following chapter will show how this conceptual framework can serve as a foundation for understanding the contributions of learning variables which ordinarily would be thought to be outside the framework of psychoanalysis.

3

INTEGRATION OF THE METAPSYCHOLOGICAL POINTS OF VIEW WITH THE LEARNING VARIABLES

A. The Dynamic Point of View

The dynamic point of view emphasizes the drives as the determinants of behavior and the changes the drives undergo as a result of the counterforces which modify them. In this section I will consider the relationships between drives, defenses, and variables as they are recognized within operant learning theory.

Let us examine the simplest case first: direct drive gratification. The oral drive is a component of the sexual drive and is known in part by its aim and object. Its aim is oral discharge, which is accomplished through sucking movements, and its object is the mother or a mother substitute. The conception of the oral drive, however, could be expanded to include not only gratification associated with the muscles around the mouth, but more generally stimulation associated with physical contact and closeness between the infant and its primary object, the mother.

The relationship between the oral drive and reinforcing stimuli is implicit in the definition of the oral drive. The mother, the object, is a reinforcer because she makes herself, or objects perceived as part of herself, available for sucking, touching, etc. She may not always function as a reinforcer, or only certain aspects of her may function as a reinforcer, depending upon which of her activities or aspects are associated with gratification. Generally, however, the drive which defines an aim and object of gratification in essence also defines reinforcers. The same analysis would hold true for other partial drives at other stages of development.

Besides reinforcing stimuli, there are discriminative stimuli which control responses. The discriminative stimulus is defined by characteristics of the drive object. It is likely that only in the mother's presence will the infant receive oral gratification. The mere appearance of the mother can therefore become a discriminative stimulus; it raises the possibility that oral gratification will take place. Other stimuli associated with the mother may serve as discriminative stimuli, such as the sound of her footsteps, certain colors, or a particular kind of smile. The discriminative stimuli can be quite complex. Finer and finer discriminations depend on the richness and complexity of the stimuli and the infant's developing capacity for finer discriminations.

The group of responses influenced by these discriminative and reinforcing stimuli can be defined as oral responses. In the simplest case, these are the responses of the infant which have as their consequence oral gratification. If sucking yields oral pleasure, then sucking responses are defined as oral responses. The infant's holding his mother, reaching for the bottle or the breast, smiling, are all associated with the pleasurable act of sucking and therefore can also be defined as oral responses.

The partial oral drive can therefore define reinforcers, discriminative stimuli, and responses. The tension created by the drive's striving for discharge not only motivates certain behaviors—crying, kicking, rubbing, or other movement—but also defines an object whose actions will further modify these behaviors. Thus we have the behaviors stimulated from within by the drives and further shaped or modified by the behavior of the drive object, that is, the reinforcer.

The behavior of the drive object has always been considered important, especially for the progressive internal regulation of behavior. This behavior of the drive object has usually been in the context of a gratifier, frustrater, limit-setter, boundary-definer, or stimulator. Viewed as a reinforcer, however, the drive object can be seen to have a further effect. For example, if the mother responds with feeding the infant only as a consequence of his kicking the crib, *kicking* will be reinforced. Of a whole series of diffuse responses such as kicking, crying, and smiling, kicking will be selected as the response which leads to being fed. To take the example one step further, kicking and head-banging and other responses which have as their characteristic some physical pain to the infant may be the ones that the mother responds to. In that case the infant learns that self-inflicted pain results in oral gratification. An aspect of the frequency and resistance of this behavior to change may be that the mother reinforces these behaviors on a schedule which both maintains the behavior at a high rate and makes it resistant to change. Later on it will be shown how such early behaviors could be developed into a broad characteristic pattern which would form an important part of the personality.

DEFENSES

More complicated is the case in which the drives are modified by counterforces, altering either their aim, their object, or both. The drives push for discharge. The counterforce of the defense alters this force. Out of this interaction arises a secondary motivation leading to behavior which offers some compromise or partial gratification.

Once the secondary motivation is identified, it can be treated in the same manner as was primary motivation in the example of the head-banging baby. The secondary motivation defines types of gratification and therefore also identifies or defines reinforcing stimuli. Since there are numerous possibilities for the derivatives of the sexual and aggressive drives, there can be many points of gratification within any drive-defense organization. There may therefore be a number of types of reinforcers.

Let us assume a person who, as a result of certain defenses against oral strivings, has developed a series of patterns in which self-destructive behavior is emitted. Let us further assume that his self-destructive behavior has elicited a good deal of attention from particularly important drive objects. In this case gratification could occur in a number of ways. The self-destructive acts may provide autoerotic gratification if certain sensations to the body are involved. Self-directed anger or secondary masochism may provide masochistic gratification. In addition, the attention elicited by the self-destructive acts—the person might be held, cuddled, or shown a lot of concern—may gratify certain oral-erotic drive derivatives. Each of these gratifications can be defined as a potential reinforcer.

As shown in the earlier example, the identification of reinforcers leads to an identification of discriminative stimuli and relevant responses. These stimuli and responses become increasingly complex because there are a variety of reinforcers. In this example, the discriminative stimuli may be any situations associated with three types of reinforcement, such as sadistic persons and/or pain-inducing objects (masochistic gratification); the smell, sight, and/or voice of attention-giving persons (oral-object erotic gratification); physical threats and/or being alone (autoerotic gratification); plus, of course, any fantasies connected with these types of reinforcement. The self-destructive behavior may include component responses which have had as their consequence these reinforcers, such as accident-proneness responses, provoking responses, and self-stimulation responses.

After these operant variables are fully identified, it can be seen how the reinforcement and schedule of reinforcement contribute to determining the emission, frequency, and resistance to change of such complex behavior as self-destructive acts. It can also be seen how the discriminative stimuli in part determine when these behaviors will occur and set in motion the processes of reinforcement which will accompany their occurrence.

Even when drive discharge patterns become quite complex because of defenses or counterforces, it is still possible to identify what is experienced as gratification, by following the vicissitudes of the libidinal and aggressive drives. The definitions of reinforcing, discriminative stimuli and responses follow and allow us to observe the effect of these environmental variables on behavior.

B. The Genetic Point of View

The genetic point of view holds that behavior is the product of both maturational and experiential factors which interact in a sequence of developmental stages and which determine the outcome of each of these stages. Stage-specific behavior, which can be understood from the other metapsychological points of view, has an important effect on later behaviors. Later behaviors which may have here-and-now determinants are often only variations of the relatively stable complex patterns formed during the early developmental stages (Rapaport, 1959, pp. 43-45). Ready examples of such later behaviors are hysterical or obsessional patterns. The genetic point of view, therefore, adheres to the concept of specific developmental stages with specific developmental tasks and outcomes, and to the idea that during these stages broad patterns are formed which partially determine later behaviors.

The following discussion will deal only with components of certain developmental stages. The same analysis, however, can be applied to other developmental issues. The goal of this discussion is to show how the interactions of a developmental stage which often result in broad patterns influencing later behavior also define characteristic responses and reinforcing and discriminative stimuli, with similar implications for behavior. It will be shown how the stimuli which influence behavior in the present are related to the stimuli of the past in terms of the development of classes of stimuli and responses.

Each developmental stage may define reinforcing stimuli, discriminative stimuli, and characteristic responses. Particular partial drives which were shown above to define stimuli and responses are associated with certain stages of development. For example, in the oral stage, pleasure is derived predominantly from sucking. Therefore, primary and secondary reinforcers are defined around sucking. The sight, smell, or touch of the mother, or a whole series of stimuli leading up to and including the pleasurable experience, could be defined as reinforcers.[1] The partial drive associated with the developmental stage would also define discriminative stimuli. If the sound of the mother walking or talking signals the baby's feeding, and along with that the pleasure associated with sucking, then these stimuli could be termed discriminative.

The identification of relevant stimuli and responses can become more complex, however, owing to the social expectations of interactions in each of these stages. These expectations and interactions, which in part define the stage and in part follow from the physical changes of the stage, associate social and cultural patterns with the event of reinforcement.

Certain physical capacities are associated with each developmental stage. In the oral stage there is the capacity for sucking; in the anal stage, the capacity for sphincter control. The ways in which different cultures, and even families within the same culture, handle feeding or toilet training vary considerably. Occasionally the family pattern may define the beginning of a stage before the actual emergence of the physical determinants of that stage. The sociocultural patterns and their association with the maturational components of a developmental stage broaden considerably the range of what

---

[1]In addition to the stimuli that are reinforcing the behavior itself, in this case sucking too may be reinforcing.

function as reinforcing and discriminative stimuli as well as what become the responses they influence.

Analysis of the physical and sociocultural aspects of a developmental stage therefore enables us to identify complex classes of stimuli and responses. A class, oral stimuli, would be one in which the discriminative and reinforcing stimuli derive from the complex patterns dealing with oral gratification. Similarly, the complex responses associated with oral gratification could be termed the oral response class.[2]

For example, in an Indian tribe which at feeding time cooked their food in ways which generated particular smells, played special music, practiced unique physical rituals, and encouraged special behavior patterns, the children would come to associate what they smelled, heard, felt, and did with the experience of oral reinforcement. These complex sensory perceptions would then come to have reinforcing and discriminative properties and would become part of a specific class of oral reinforcing and discriminative stimuli. The complex behaviors associated with reinforcement would become part of a specific oral response class.

According to the genetic point of view, patterns formed during early developmental stages contribute to the later development of the personality; and later behavior often represents only elaborations or variations of these earlier established patterns. Operant learning theory, on the other hand, tends to view behavior as a discrete entity under discrete stimulus control and as continually open to change by a change in the relevant environmental variables. For the learning variables to be compatible with the genetic point of view, it must be shown that they can accommodate the idea that later behavior may only be part of an earlier established pattern.

It will be demonstrated how the infant's relatively undifferentiated response patterns and poor discriminative capacity influence the broadness of these stage-specific response and stimulus classes. The broadness of the classes will be seen to determine their relative effect on later behaviors.

While each stage of development influences the response and stimulus classes associated with it, in the infancy stage the *breadth* and *context* of the response and stimulus classes are influenced by the

---

[2] In operant theory, responses are defined functionally by the consequences they elicit. Thus any responses resulting in oral gratification would be considered as part of the response class, oral responses.

characteristics of infantile perception and undifferentiated response patterns. During the early phases of development, discriminative capacity may be poor and response patterns undifferentiated: the infant cannot discriminate among different stimuli or responses. Because the stimuli all seem rather similar, there is a tendency toward undifferentiated generalization[3] of stimuli. A response will be under the control of not only the stimuli that set the occasion for its reinforcement and the stimuli which reinforce the response, but also all the similar undiscriminated stimuli. Thus even though the mother is the original reinforcing agent, if the infant cannot discriminate the mother from other adults, other adults will also have reinforcing capacity. Similarly, the sound of other adults walking or talking may serve as discriminative stimuli for certain behavior. The response patterns also tend to be undifferentiated, so that there is a tendency toward generalization there as well. Various arm movements or leg movements, various facial expressions, and various internal states may all seem alike to the infant.

Consider the example of the infant whose mother came to feed him only after he banged his head on the crib, and who was thus conditioned to bang for touch or nurturance. During this early developmental stage he is unable to distinguish his mother from other people, and therefore indiscriminately associates attention from any person with touch and nurturance. Since he also perceives his own behavior undifferentiatedly, he may not be able to distinguish head-banging from any other self-punishing behavior; this could lead him to a relatively broad response class characterized by self-punishment. As he grows and develops, a wide spectrum of self-punitive behavior to get attention from *any* person may evolve.

These classes can also be formed, maintained, and further determined by differential reinforcement. Here, responses which may be topographically very different are classed together by a common feature defined by the contingencies of reinforcement.

The fact that an infant's capacity for discrimination improves as he grows does not necessarily significantly change the broad patterns of behavior and reinforcement learned earlier. The learning which occurs before there is an ability to discriminate may continue in its breadth to the degree that the early undifferentiated

[3]This is to be distinguished from the type of generalization in which discriminated differences are subsumed under more useful categories, such as in the construction of abstractions.

maladaptive patterns interfere with the establishment of new differentiated patterns. Early maladaptive reinforcers and the responses they influence can become the foundation of future broad, only slightly more differentiated, maladaptive patterns of response and reinforcement.

THE EVOLUTION OF STIMULUS AND RESPONSE CLASSES

The conceptualization of the evolution of the stimulus and response classes depends in part on our understanding of development, and the issues at various developmental stages. The organism will emit responses which are characteristic of a developmental stage and are under the influence of the stimuli of that stage, depending on how compatible these are with the responses and stimuli of the preceding stage. It is from the old ones that the new ones evolve or are shaped. For example, let us postulate that the task of the first developmental stage is trust and that of the second stage is autonomy (Erikson, 1956). Let us also say that autonomy is a differentiated form of trusting responses. If an organism is already emitting trusting responses from these responses, it can shape autonomous responses. In addition, the stimuli the mother made available to influence trusting behavior will be related to the stimuli she is making available to influence autonomous behavior. Let us say that the classes of discriminative and reinforcing stimuli which influence autonomous behavior are "respectful stimuli." The child is respected for autonomous behavior. If this respect is associated with the touch and nurturance of the first stage, it acquires a reinforcing capacity. The child's potential for increasing his discriminative capacity is developing because of the maturation of his central nervous system, resulting in more sharply defined stimulus and response classes. Thus we have a slowly developing organism whose responses and the stimuli which influence them build on one another. The resulting picture is similar to the psychoanalytic concept of layering of the personality. The behavior at the core becomes slowly elaborated and differentiated in each subsequent layer.

To complete the example, consider what happens if in the oral stage mistrusting, rather than trusting, behaviors predominate. It is possible that autonomous behavior (that is, the second stage) cannot be differentiated from mistrusting behavior and, in fact, might be incompatible with it. Similarly, just as adaptive responses cannot be differentiated from nonadaptive ones, it may be that the maladaptive behavior necessarily remains under the control of early generalized reinforcers. Mistrusting responses would not only remain in the behavioral repertory but would remain under the influence of the poorly discriminated oral reinforcers. This process is seen when a patient's behavior is altered, but left under the control of the same general reinforcers. The results may be short-lived.

Why adaptive responses and developmentally advanced reinforcers often do not naturally evolve from maladaptive responses and early generalized reinforcers should be explored in more detail.

In operant experiments new behaviors can only be learned from already existing behaviors. If a pigeon is to be taught to push a lever, this differentiated response will arise from already existing responses, such as standing near the lever and making diffuse movements toward it. The initial capricious pressing of the lever will then be selectively reinforced and a new differentiated behavior begun. The pigeon must, of course, be neurologically capable of making the lever-pressing movement or no amount of differential reinforcement will help him achieve this behavior.

In a child, trusting responses may include such responses as the comfortable holding of the mother, the comfortable play with her, and the comfortable exploration of his crib. From these initial trusting responses, in conjunction with greater motor capacity, autonomous responses, such as the relaxed movement away from the mother, the exploration of his home, and the comfortable touching of new objects, may evolve. It is possible to see how the comfortable touching of the crib and the mother might, with appropriate reinforcement, lead to the comfortable touching of new objects.

From the perspective of the feelings which accompany these behaviors and may also be conceptualized as responses, it is possible to see how the infant who trusts his environment and trusts himself will probably begin to explore his environment autonomously, that is, without the mother's constant help, in conjunction with the age-appropriate maturation of his central nervous system, because such behavior is within his developing capacity and not hindered significantly by painful experiences or overwhelming fears. As this autonomous behavior is reinforced by the child's discoveries and the mother's selective encouragement and demonstrated enjoyment of his new capacities, it becomes more established in the behavioral repertory.

Where there is mistrusting behavior at the first stage of development, the evolution of autonomous behavior may be compromised. Mistrusting responses may include responses such as fearful clinging, tantrums, and continuous self-stimulation. From these basic responses, it would be difficult to shape such autonomous responses as comfortable exploration and touching. Even with the maturational capacity for responses such as leaving the mother's side, the response repertory may not contain the responses from which new, autonomous responses could emerge. From the perspective of the feelings which accompany these behaviors, the child's basic mistrust of the environment may also hamper his using his capacity. If attempts to leave the mother's side result in painful affects such as fear, or in painful experiences such as the mother's getting angry, or in the reinforcement of incompatible behavior such as the mother cuddling him to keep him at her side, the possibility for autonomous behavior will be further compromised. These latter circumstances in part depend on the continuation into the next stage of development of the type of experiences which led to the initial state of mistrust.

The maturational capacity for new autonomous behaviors may be present, but the earlier established response classes do not provide the base for the development of new response patterns. There is a discontinuity between maturational capacity and the capacity for the development of new adaptive responses. This results in an evolution of responses along a new line of development, which is determined by a compromise between the new maturational capacities and the limiting early maladaptive response patterns. The new line of response development retains the early maladaptive response patterns at its base. In normal development, where there is an accord between maturation and adaptive response development, these early patterns give way to more advanced ones. Usually these processes occur by degrees rather than in an all-or-nothing fashion.

The issue of how reinforcers and discriminative stimuli evolve and are differentiated is more complex. In operant experiments new reinforcers and discriminative stimuli can be developed by being paired with already established reinforcers. If a bell is paired with food, the bell will achieve a reinforcing capacity. This reinforcing capacity will depend on the reinforcing capacity of the food and the continued occasional presentation of food paired with the bell. The bell, or new conditioned reinforcer in this situation, hardly functions independently.

Another procedure for changing reinforcers and discriminative stimuli is shading. If a red light serves as a discriminative stimulus or conditioned reinforcer and one wishes to have a triangle serve as the discriminative stimulus or conditioned reinforcer instead, one can present the red light with a triangle drawn on it. Then one can slowly dim the red light. At some point the triangle, which will gradually emerge in more detail as the light dims, will take over as the relevant stimulus and have the discriminative or reinforcing properties of the red light. Something like this shading procedure may occur when a mother begins to withdraw her breast and wean her child. Slowly other properties, characteristics of the mother, may come into greater prominence, and her total person, rather than just a part of her, takes on discriminative and reinforcing properties.

However, in this procedure, as in the earlier one, the new stimulus, if it is to serve as a reinforcer, must maintain an attachment to an original unconditioned reinforcer. There is still a pairing or association between two stimuli. While the new discriminative stimulus may take over completely from the one that has faded out, the new reinforcer which emerges through this type of pairing will maintain its efficacy only by its occasional association with the primary reinforcer.

Operant learning models therefore have only little to contribute to the explanation of how reinforcers change and evolve. For example, why certain reinforcers are efficacious at certain stages of development and not at others, and why in successful psychotherapy a patient may experience a change in what he experiences as some of his major reinforcers, are not considered within the operant learning models.

This fact should not be considered a deficiency of operant learning theory, since these phenomena are not of major interest to it. Within operant approaches, reinforcers are empirically identified or experimentally created, e.g., hunger. The major focus is on their functional relationships with behavior.

However, for a psychoanalytic developmental learning model that can integrate components of operant learning theory, the is-

sue of the evolution and change of reinforcers is central. Psychoanalytic drive theory conceptualizes the vicissitudes of the drives
through the different stages of development. In healthy development, early drive organizations do not disappear, but recede in
importance and are integrated with the drive organizations of
later stages. The oral, anal, and phallic drive organizations are integrated under the supremacy of the genital organization. The
same process occurs for stage-specific reinforcers. Older reinforcers recede in importance and are integrated with the reinforcers of the genital organization. The existing drive organization
will define the currently operative reinforcers. In normal development, therefore, as maturational changes define new stages of development, the reinforcers change as well. In addition, as
discriminatory capacity improves, responses and their reinforcers
become more differentiated.

An important question is, in what circumstances do early reinforcers retain their influence at the expense of the evolution and
differentiation of later reinforcers? While the capacity for new reinforcers develops with maturation, for this capacity to be realized, the new reinforcers must be capable of being paired with
earlier ones. While in the experimental situation the efficacy of
the new reinforcer continues to rest on its relationship to the old
one, in human development, new maturational capacities lead to
the new reinforcer's eventually having an independent reinforcing
capacity. Nevertheless, the pairing aspect of this process is quite
necessary at the initial stage of the establishment of a new reinforcer. It provides continuity between reinforcers and thereby
gives impetus to the new reinforcers. More important, the pairing
permits a relative relinquishment of the earlier reinforcer. Because the new reinforcer is paired with the old one, it provides
both the new and the old type of gratification. This permits the
slow relinquishing of the old, as the new type of gratification gains
impetus from the new maturational capacities. For example, initially merely the experience of the mother's presence nearby may
function as a reinforcer for a child. For the reinforcer to shift to
the experience of her approval, a specific and more differentiated
type of "presence," the child must relinquish aspects of the original
reinforcer. This is facilitated by the child's growing discrimination
of his mother's reactions in conjunction with his ability to
relinquish his need for her total presence. The continuity between a

warm accepting total presence and approval makes it possible for him initially to connect the gratification of her total presence with her approval. As he becomes able to maintain a representation of her in accord with new maturational capacities, he is able to relinquish his need for her total presence and respond more to her approval. At some time in this process, the continuity of her presence with her approval, their compatible simultaneous presence, makes it possible for the approval to function as a conditioned reinforcer until maturational reinforcers, in conjunction with experience, give it a relatively independent reinforcing capacity.

The successful weaning of a child may involve a similar process. The breast or its substitute, i.e., a part of the mother, is the initial reinforcer. With the capacity to perceive other aspects of his mother and integrate some of them into his image of her, the child may be reinforced by these more integrated perceptions. For the perception of the mother as a whole to become independently reinforcing, the primary reinforcement of the breast must be somewhat relinquished. The continuity between the two stimulus configurations, *breast* and *whole mother,* will permit *whole mother* to provide both types of reinforcement and thereby allows a slow relinquishing of the breast in accord with new development. This is similar to the fading-out procedure described earlier; only in this case the fading out of the breast in favor of the total person is facilitated by maturation.

This argument is developed to account for the unusual case in which the environment may be open to using new reinforcers in accord with development. As indicated, most environments which facilitate mistrusting behavior with aversive oral reinforcement are unlikely to change and offer new, more adaptive reinforcers. The continuation of the old types of reinforcers would obviously further consolidate the processes described.

Maladaptive behavior patterns may also interfere with the evolution of reinforcers. When early generalized reinforcers are maintaining maladaptive patterns, such as generalized attention-maintaining self-destructive behavior, the patterns, in this case the self-destructive behavior, may also interfere with the relinquishing of the early reinforcers.

A child involved in self-destructive patterns who relates to others in a mistrustful manner is unlikely to invest all his chances for reinforcement in a few select persons. He is equally unlikely to develop behavior which will elicit intense gratification from a few select persons. For example, in normal development a child switches from being reinforced by generalized nurturance to being reinforced by the mother's generalized nurturance to being reinforced by the mother's approval, a specific kind of nurturance. This evolution and differentiation will depend not only on maturational capacities but on the existence of adaptive response patterns which generate an emotional climate in which the pairing of stimuli is possible and older reinforcers are relinquished. This is most clearly seen in the studies of institutionalized children who have experienced early deprivation and who are later promiscuous in their object relationships and sources of gratification (generalized and undifferentiated reinforcers).

This discussion has emphasized how early responses and reinforcers can in certain situations maintain their importance at the expense of developmentally more advanced responses and reinforcers. An aspect of this process which requires further examination is the breadth of these patterns and/or their lack of differentiation. While the continuation of an early pattern into later life is maladaptive, such a continuation in a broad and undifferentiated state is even more maladaptive.

Except in severe cases of physical or emotional insult, maturational capacities for such processes as the development of motor skills, a hierarchy of libidinal interests, and cognition unfold in a predetermined sequence. As indicated, whether these capacities fully develop and how they develop will depend in part on the earlier established responses and reinforcers they evolve from.

However, the breadth or degree of differentiation of these patterns will depend primarily on one aspect of their development: their development in relationship to human objects. Responses can be emitted in relationship to human objects or in relationship to the self or inanimate objects. Reinforcement can come from a human object, from the self, or from inanimate objects.

In order for the child's discriminatory capacity—such as the capacity to know the mother from other adults and later to know her approval from her disapproval and her love from her anger—to increase as he grows older, he must develop a primary attachment to the mother. He must develop an intimate relationship with her in order to develop these discriminatory capacities because only an intimate human relationship can provide the differential consequences necessary for this type of discriminative learning. It is doubtful that these discriminative capacities could be developed in relation to inanimate objects. While they may in part be developed in relation to the self, they would certainly be compromised.

When maladaptive responses are under the influence of maladaptive undifferentiated reinforcers, this pairing of reinforcers may either not occur or occur in a way that will not lead to developmentally more advanced reinforcers. A mother who is reinforcing her infant's self-destructive behavior is probably doing so with a somewhat aversive or painful type of attention or nurturance. Loving, accepting, respectful attention would not be likely to evolve from the painful attention. The stimulus configurations, which probably have different respondents associated with them, are too different to provide the continuity which would result in pairing. This explanation assumes that the mother who is providing aversive attention is capable of switching to loving, respectful attention. In reality, however, this is often not the case.

Whatever evolution of reinforcers takes place would be along its own unique line. This line would have the early maladaptive reinforcers at its foundation. Normal maturation, which would ordinarily provide an impetus toward the evolution of adaptive, developmentally advanced reinforcers, could not as effectively provide that impetus here because of the lack of stimulus continuity and the nonrelinquishing of the older reinforcers. A different line would be started. Without the full integration of this maturational impetus, early generalized maladaptive reinforcers will maintain a position of primacy and will affect the organization of developmentally later reinforcers. For example, in the situation of mistrusting behavior under the control of generalized aversive oral stimuli, the stimuli would not have continuity with the loving respect which is usually associated with autonomous behavior. The combined force of stimulus continuity and maturational impetus is not available to facilitate the relinquishing of early reinforcers in favor of later ones. The new line of development is therefore influenced by the earlier reinforcers.

The capacity to distinguish the mother from other adults develops because this capacity is reinforced by the mother's gratification. When the infant recognizes the mother, the mother reacts to him. His response (recognition) is selectively reinforced. Through the process of differential reinforcement, he learns that other adults feel, smell, or look different. The development of the capacity to differentiate the mother's approval from her disapproval would occur in a similar manner. This capacity is selectively reinforced because it leads to responses which have as their consequence differential reactions from the mother. When the child first walks unaided, the mother may pick him up and smile and hold him warmly. If he knocks over her favorite piece of china, the mother may yell and slap his hand. These different behaviors of the child's which elicit different consequences from the mother (differential positive and negative reinforcement) facilitate the development of his maturational capacities.

Under the influence of aversive generalized reinforcers, the early development of mistrustful responses is likely to compromise the early attachment to the primary object. The first discrimination between the mother and the self and the mother and others may not be optimally developed. Mistrustful behavior toward the mother may then compromise the establishment of an intimate relationship in which the optimal differential reinforcement necessary for the child's further development of his discriminative capacity can occur. For example, the mistrustful child may frequently not be gratified by the mother's approval and therefore may not be optimally open to object-related differential reinforcement. This is to say nothing of the fact that the mother is not likely to alter the nature of her behavior and suddenly become sensitive to her child's needs, offering him the type of differential reinforcement which would foster his development. Object-related discriminations may therefore not be fully developed.

To illustrate this situation, consider the case of a child whose maturational capacities unfold but who does not have the proper object relationships to foster the development of discrimination. This child may demonstrate the development of new libidinal zones with a change in areas of self-stimulation. He may show greater motor capacity in his dexterity with inanimate objects. However, his ability to discriminate or respond to complex inner emotional cues or cues from another person may remain relatively undifferentiated. This lack of differentiation can, of course, occur in all degrees from the most extreme to the almost imperceptible.

It has been shown how early maladaptive patterns of responses and reinforcement may remain in the personality because of a lack of response and stimulus continuity with developmentally advanced patterns. It has also been shown how the retention of these early patterns may interfere with the type of object relationship necessary for optimal development of discriminative capacity. The maintenance of broad early patterns of response and reinforcements compromises the development of later patterns. The aspects of maturation that continue become organized under the primacy of these earlier patterns. In this way, genital pleasures may be part of earlier organizations. At any level of organization the establishment of maladaptive patterns may lead to processes which compromise later development.

The formation of broad classes of responses and influencing stimuli has implications for the frequency and maintenance of certain characteristic behavioral patterns. If the stimulus class is broad, there is a greater probability that its component stimuli will be present in any given environment. This is true for both discriminative and reinforcing stimuli. Thus, if *any* person is a discriminative stimulus for a particular behavioral pattern, we can expect this pattern to be emitted frequently, since a person is present in most settings. If any type of attention is a positive reinforcer, we can expect a behavior pattern under its influence to be reinforced at least some of the time, as attention in the most general sense is fairly easy to elicit. Similarly, the broader the response class, the higher the probability that one of the responses in that class is being emitted and positively reinforced at any given time. Therefore, broad behavior patterns under the influence of broad discriminative and reinforcing stimulus classes are relatively permanent parts of the behavioral repertory.

To illustrate, persons under the control of generalized attention reinforcers will seek sexual attention or respectful attention in the context of more general gratification, such as oral gratification. We often assume that such persons had difficulties early in their lives and that their main problems are grounded in early developmental issues. They tend to be resistant to change, and what is often defined as change is usually only a variation on a more basic theme. Emotionally they do not discriminate between different types of attention and therefore may have difficulty in adjusting to average expectable social environments. Conversely, more differentiated persons are influenced by more specific stimuli and have more specific and flexible behavioral repertories.

The interactions that occur during each developmental stage not only serve to define specific broad patterns which may determine aspects of the individual personality but also serve to define specific broad classes of responses and reinforcing and discriminative stimuli. The assignment of stimuli and responses into broad classes allows us to identify these variables in natural settings and then use the concepts of operant learning theory to see how these variables work back on behavior further to shape and modify it.

THE ROLE OF DISRUPTIVE ANXIETY IN RELATION TO DISCRIMINATORY CAPACITY

Before continuing to the economic point of view, it is reasonable to speculate about the role of disruptive anxiety in relation to the influence of one's discriminative capacity on the specificity of his stimulus and response classes.

It is frequently noticed that under the influence of intense anxiety, an adult will not discriminate as well as he does normally. This process is occasionally referred to as an ego regression secondary to anxiety. Perhaps during early development, behaviors learned during states of disruptive anxiety are learned with poorer discriminatory capacity than other behaviors of the same stage that are learned during calm states. From this we could build a theory to explain the relative rigidity and staying power of maladaptive behaviors associated with this type of anxiety as compared to the more adaptive behaviors associated with calm states. For example, if an infant learns to throw a tantrum when he is feeling frustrated, it may be that his behavior is learned during a state of intense anxiety and, therefore, his discriminatory capacity is not as great as it is at other times during this particular developmental phase. Thus the response class "tantrum" and the stimuli which would come to influence this response class would tend to become broader than other response classes and stimuli of this same stage.

This analysis provides an explanation for the unevenness of development as determined by the relative changes in discriminatory capacity and has interesting implications for symptom formation and certain character pathology. For example, the child who witnesses parental sexual intercourse and experiences disruptive anxiety, and then denies his perception to deal with his anxiety, may, owing to his reduced discriminatory capacity, generalize the use of denial. This mechanism would then play a significant role in his developing character. Similarly, in traumatic neuroses, the intense anxiety that accompanies the learning of these maladaptive patterns may reduce discriminatory capacity, leading to the formation of broad stimulus and response classes. The responses thereby tend to remain in the repertory. It is interesting that techniques used to treat traumatic neurosis, such as Amytal interview, tend to alter discriminatory capacity. Psychoanalytic treatment, too, over a longer period of time, allows the patient, via the formation of the transference, to operate temporarily with an altered discriminatory capacity. In this way he can deal with memories and behaviors at the same level of generalization as the one at which they were learned. Discriminations are encouraged at various points of analytic treatment as well, and discriminatory capacity may improve in certain areas. In general, there is a balance between reduced discriminatory capacity to facilitate the discovery of conflicts and increased discriminatory capacity to foster relearning.

C. The Economic Point of View

The economic point of view deals with the energic aspects of mental phenomena. Because of its complexity and the divergent opinions regarding its utility, this point of view will be discussed only in relation to the learning variables and the understanding it provides in addition to the other points of view. It focuses on the quantitative aspect of the force behind various aspects of mental functioning. For example, there can be increases or decreases in drive tension, such as those at puberty or menopause. Certain fixations and drive defense organizations play a prominent role in the personality, and in that sense contain a relatively greater amount of libidinal and aggressive energy than those that play a lesser role in the personality. Relative capacities and flexibility of autonomous and defensive functions, as well as more generally the capacity for attending to the outer world versus the need for regulation of the inner world, can all be conceptualized within the context of energy distribution or economic terms: exchanges between drive energies, and neutralized energies.

In terms of behavior, we can characterize the economic point of view as emphasizing the prominence of certain behaviors in relation to others. If a symptom has a great deal of energy associated with it, it may be quite prominent, tenacious, or even permanent within the personality. Similarly, if a good deal of energy is bound up in character resistances to certain impulses, we might see inflexible, repetitive defensive behavior.

A particularly important aspect of the economic point of view is fixation. The concept of fixation implies an attachment of energy to particular mental phenomena at various stages during development. The amount of energy attached has an important bearing on the influence of behaviors at a given stage on later behaviors. For example, libido fixated during the anal stage decreases the amount of libido which can progress to the genital organizational level.

The concept from operant learning theory which most closely approximates the economic point of view is the deprivation-satiation operation. A deprivation operation involves limiting the person's exposure to a certain positive reinforcer. This deprivation of the reinforcer leads to a multiplication of its effects. If a baby who is fed each time he cries is deprived of the food reinforcer, the behavior—crying—which is under the control of this reinforcer consequently occurs more frequently. This increase in the frequency of crying is a direct effect of the deprivation operation and should not be confused with increases in the frequency of certain behaviors due to other variables, such as a change in a schedule of reinforcement. Such deprivations can also increase behavior which is not directly associated with obtaining the withheld reinforcer. A satiation operation works in converse fashion. If one is satiated with food, food's reinforcing efficacy may be decreased. The similarity of the processes defined by the economic point of view and by a deprivation-satiation operation lies in the fact that both can determine the relative dominance or tenacity of a behavioral pattern: the economic point of view in terms of energy distribution, the deprivation-satiation operation in terms of stimulus efficacy.

Yet the conception of a deprivation-satiation operation hardly accounts for the complex phenomena that the economic point of view can accommodate. The following discussion will further develop the conception of the deprivation-satiation operation so that it can accommodate more complex phenomena.

Hypothetically, an infant can be considered to be more or less deprived of those reinforcers which he cannot provide for himself. He will increase the frequency of behavior associated with obtaining certain reinforcers to the degree that he is deprived of them. Since during each stage of development the reinforcers tend to be stage-specific, the infant would tend to be deprived of the reinforcers of that stage. Deprivation is therefore a stage-specific concept.

It is plausible to assume that, if a stage-specific problem is not mastered, there will be a continuous deprivation of, and therefore striving for, the reinforcers associated with that stage. For example, if an infant is deprived of the gratification associated with the oral stage of development, he may, during subsequent stages, continue to learn those behaviors which lead to oral gratification or reinforcement rather than those which lead to normal stage-specific reinforcement. The increased efficacy of the withheld reinforcers as well as the increased frequency of behaviors associated with them compromises the development of more advanced behaviors and reinforcers. Even with the maturational ascendancy of anal reinforcers, the increased efficacy of and seeking for oral reinforcers associated with oral deprivation would compromise their development. Normal maturation is therefore impaired; the resulting personality would tend to be rigid and controlled not only by early generalized reinforcers but also by a constant state of deprivation.

Satiation could have similar effects in a number of other directions. A child who is satiated with the reinforcers of a particular stage might not develop the behaviors necessary to obtain those particular types of reinforcers later in life. For example, if an infant were constantly given food without manifesting any behavior, the behaviors which lead to getting food or, later, attention, caring, or love, might not be developed. Instead there might be a constant set of expectations for being given to. The infant would have learned that passivity leads to gratification. In this case there is a response class paucity, as well as a constant state of deprivation. Responses which could maintain reinforcement have not been learned.

The concept of a deprivation-satiation operation is also related to economic considerations of personality flexibility in terms of shifts of energies for different endeavors. Consider the person with an alcohol problem. His maladaptive response classes are under the control of oral reinforcers, of which there are two types: self-oral reinforcement (drinking), and object oral reinforcement (obtaining very primitive kinds of nurturing attention). Since this person is in a constant state of deprivation because he was deprived of oral reinforcement during his oral stage, he manifests a high frequency of behavior which has as its consequence these types of reinforcement. When this person is deprived of oral social reinforcement, his drinking behavior increases, and when he is deprived of alcohol, his dependency-seeking behavior increases. The shift in his behavior is between his two oral responses rather than between these and developmentally more advanced ones. Thus if the influencing stimuli—the alcohol and a person who can nurture him—have a good deal of efficacy because of the alcoholic's earlier deprivation, the behaviors under their control are quite permanent, and severely limit the flexibility of his behavioral repertory.

In part, to talk about a deprivation-satiation operation is just one way to consider differing states of drive tension. Indeed, states of drive tension might be the internal counterparts of these external events. The particular value of this concept, however, lies in its focus on directly observable environmental events which can be studied experimentally and on which a wealth of information has already been collected. Application of this concept can give us additional information about the determinants of change in drive tension and their implications for changes in behavior.

For example, we know that an obsessional symptom is in one sense behavior that results from the libidinization of a mental process. The degree of libidinization will influence the symptom's tenacity and its recurrence. At the same time we can evaluate the efficacy of the environmental stimuli which are also exerting control over this obsessional symptom: They can independently shape, modify, and make it resistant to change. There is an interaction between the energic determinants of this symptom and their environmental counterparts. That the energic determinants of behavior are related to the efficacy of the relevant environmental stimuli leads to an additional question: What is the energic counterpart to behavioral change that follows differential reinforcement with these environmental stimuli? Another way to phrase this question is: What type of energy shift, if any, takes place in behavioral change without insight?

Consider a traditional reinforcement procedure. A desired behavior is selectively reinforced while its undesired counterpart is purposely nonreinforced: It is extinguished.

Since positive reinforcement is similar to gratification, one behavior leads to regular gratification while another does not. During development, gratification leads to energy being attached to the mental representations associated with that gratification. The concept of fixation is an extreme case. Overgratification leads to a large amount of energy being attached to a mental phenomenon. During development, then, gratification of a behavioral pattern leads to energy being attached to that pattern. Similarly, selective reinforcement of a new behavioral pattern would have as its counterpart the libidinization of the representation of that pattern. The increase in frequency of reinforced behaviors, therefore, has its economic counterpart.

But where does this energy come from? With behavioral change that occurs through insight, the energy that attaches to new behavior comes from the energy that is freed from its defensive use.

In change due to differential reinforcement, the energy that attaches to the new behaviors comes from the old or undesirable behaviors which are extinguished. The rationale for this energy transformation is as follows. In order for energy to remain attached to a behavioral pattern, there must be some occasional gratification of that pattern. This statement is derived from Rapaport's concept of stimulus nutriment (Rapaport, 1958). He maintains that structures need some stimulus nutriment (reinforcement) to maintain their integrity. When a structure is destructuralized, energy is detached from it. Similarly, a behavioral pattern which was once gratified but is then selectively not gratified will lose its energy. This energy then becomes available for the new reinforced behavior.

It is important to note that this is an energy transformation in only one direction, from one behavioral pattern to another. The goal of psychoanalysis is usually an energy transformation in two directions: a shift to new behaviors and a shift upward in the developmental level of the libidinal and aggressive energy, e.g., oral or anal to phallic to genital levels. This two-directional energy shift accounts for behavioral change in the context of general personality growth. The transformation of energy described for reinforcement change is a change in behavior but at a constant level of development. If the libido is basically oral in quality, it will be "oral" libido that will attach to the new behaviors. In other words, the behavior changes, but what is sought after or experienced as gratifying remains the same. A maturational shift, which would involve a shift in what is experienced as reinforcing, could not be accounted for in operant theory.

One example of the value of conceptualizing reinforcement in terms of an attachment of energy is in understanding aspects of the relationship between a fixation and a pattern of gratification. While it is known that there are differences in the rigidity of fixations, there is no way to conceptualize all the factors which contribute to these differences. Different patterns of gratification can be conceptualized as reinforcement schedules. Each schedule has its own implications for the resistance to change of behavior. For example, the variable interval schedule leads to resistant behavior, while the continuous schedule leads to relatively easy-to-change behavior. The concept of the schedule of reinforcement therefore provides a model in which not only the quantity of gratification but its pattern can be seen to have specific relationships to the characteristics of a fixation. The implications of the concept of the schedule of reinforcement will be developed and illustrated in Chapter 6. Here it can be mentioned that types of mothering could be studied to see if certain patterns involved in the mothering experience approximate certain schedules of reinforcement. Hypotheses might be generated; for example, inconsistent gratification, which approximates a variable interval schedule, leads to a more rigid fixation than continuous overgratification, which approximates a continuous schedule.

D. THE STRUCTURAL POINT OF VIEW

The structural hypothesis originated, according to Rapaport (1959), when "it was observed that drives do not unequivocally determine behavior in general nor symptom formation in particular. In contrast to the drive processes, whose rate of change is fast and whose course is paroxysmal, the factors which conflict with them and codetermine behavior appeared to be invariant, or at least slower to change" (p. 53). The hypothesis of the id, ego, and superego as the three structures of the personality has become more complex with the recognition of structure building, the structural role of identifications, the role of the ego's defensive substructures, substructures to do with orienting, processing, and executive controls, and the conception of relatively autonomous structures (Rapaport, 1959, p. 54).

To understand the implications of the structural hypothesis for the operant learning variables and vice versa, it is important to consider the concept of structure in more general functional terms.

The term *structure* is a metaphor intended to help us organize our thinking about behavior. The concept of internal structure as a mediator is useful only insofar as it enables certain inferences to be made about the stability of this mediator and its relationship to very general and basic areas of functioning. The presence of these mediators may be inferred from observable behaviors.

Another way to examine this matter is temporarily to set the metaphor aside and deal directly with those observations which we use to construct the metaphor—the first-order observations. We could say that structures are superordinate response classes. These response classes are simply broader and *more* superordinate than those responses we call behavior.[4]

The function of synthesis, for example, and the structures which mediate this function, can be conceived as a superordinate response class having a complex series of responses with a common goal. Within this organization, substructures dealing with thinking, defense, and rational action can be thought of as more specific response classes. Specific thoughts or actions (e.g., attempting to free associate to solve a problem) are specific responses used in the service of these broader classes. These response classes or responses may come under stimulus control, that is, be reinforced. The reinforcement may occur under differing schedules, which will have implications for their stability and the manner in which they exhibit their function. This matter will be clarified later (see Chapter 6).

---

[4]A lack of distinction in defining what level of classes one is talking about has made the comparison between psychodynamic therapy and behavioral therapy difficult to assess, as in theory each functions at a different level. Even though behavioral theorists talk of their results as generalizing into other areas, they are still dealing with relatively smaller, more discrete response classes than is the psychodynamic therapist, who purports to deal with the most general classes of behavior, such as structures.

Just as we can conceive of superordinate response classes, so can we conceive of related stimulus classes. The experiential (stimulus class) organization is the organization of the person's responsiveness to the environmental stimuli which influence behavior. In learning-theory terms, what the person experiences as rewarding or pleasurable, or unrewarding or unpleasurable, is called the class of influencing stimuli; that is, the discriminative and reinforcing stimuli.

The vicissitudes of this variable are exemplified by a person's experiencing a change in what is reinforcing for him. Consider a hospitalized patient who experiences generalized attention as reinforcing. If this patient changes and is no longer reinforced by generalized attention but only by respectful attention, upon leaving the hospital he will be able to obtain respect only by highly selected and differentiated behavior, including work and the establishment of mature relationships. If what is reinforcing is altered, he will be in a situation in which selective, highly differentiated "mature behavioral patterns" will be maintained by the natural contingencies of reinforcement in natural settings. If, on the other hand, his behaviors change but he is still gratified by generalized attention, he may find he obtains generalized gratification with maladaptive behaviors, such as getting drunk. A change in what is experienced as pleasurable or gratifying can be conceived as being related to structuralized patterns of drive organization. As indicated in the discussion of the dynamic point of view, the drives can interact with defenses, giving rise to secondary motivations which then determine what is reinforcing. These drive patterns can become structuralized, or can determine superordinate stimulus classes.

This important variable, the nature or class of the reinforcer which controls behavior, is often overlooked in learning theory's focus on behavior. One could raise the question: Which is more relevant, changing behavior, or changing what will be reinforcing? If what is reinforcing is changed, rules or requirements for new behavior are set up anyway. To receive the gratification of mature love, for instance, requires highly differentiated behavioral patterns. Of course, the behavioral repertory capable of eliciting such reinforcement must exist.[5]

[5]This issue touches on a developmental aspect of behavior which is central to psychoanalytic theory but not central to operant learning theory, whose models focus on the functional relationships between stimulus and response rather than on their specific organization in different human beings.

Within learning theory, the reinforcers have usually been treated empirically. New reinforcers are created through their association with old reinforcers. Nevertheless, the older reinforcers still maintain their reinforcing capacity, and, in fact, are the very foundation upon which the new reinforcers rest. They are therefore far from losing their power. When we talk of altering what will be a reinforcer, though, we are talking about altering something within the organism's capacities for pleasure. We are talking about something seemingly inside that learning theorists have treated empirically or assumed to be innate, or more precisely, in terms of their experimental analyses, treated as "givens." Yet, as was indicated, we can conceptualize what will be reinforcing in terms of superordinate stimulus classes related to patterns of drive organization.[6]

As we observe a person and how the various components of his psychic structure are dynamically related to each other, we can similarly appreciate the relationships between various response and stimulus classes. For example, just as separate structures can interact in conflict-forming new organizations, such as compromise formations, separate response and stimulus classes can interact to form new response and stimulus classes.

Consider a person with relatively good ego functioning. Most of the time his behavior reflects a high level of synthesis which is in accord with adaptation. His ego functions are reinforced both internally and externally. He maintains a high level of self-esteem and is successful in his interactions with his environment. But he suddenly moves into an environment (e.g., the army) in which drive derivatives are reinforced. Now behavior directly related to pregenital drive derivatives pushes for expression, and his ego functions, ordinarily able to synthesize these drive derivatives with other demands, are overwhelmed. Vacillations in his behavior appear; there are expressions of drive and self-condemnation,

[6]As an example, this conceptualization of structure in terms of classes of responses and stimuli can be applied to the controversy between behaviorists and dynamic therapists over what constitutes real change: Which is more important, the behavior or the underlying cause? It is possible to consider this disagreement in terms of the broadness of the classes and their relationship to each other. Does the therapist wish to intervene in the broad general classes, or in the more specific narrow classes? Are the changed behaviors merely different forms of old, general maladaptive response classes and under the influence of the same general reinforcers, such as symptomatic change, or are they part of new, broad response classes and under the influence of new, more differentiated reinforcers, as in structural change?

as well as attempts at a better synthesis. In this illustration the selective reinforcement of drive derivatives contributed to a conflict between these behaviors and the response classes derived from certain ego functions.

An interaction between an increase in drive tension and ego processes results in new levels of organization and equilibrium, often in compromise formations. New or different response and stimulus classes are established.

Consider what occurs during a regressive movement. A regression from the genital level of organization to a pregenital level results in a series of changes. The drive organization changes. Earlier formed defenses may be called into operation. In response to these changes, the ego adjusts with its own organizational changes. In learning terms, these shifts result in the formation of different stimulus and response classes. The person is behaving differently, and what he experiences as gratifying is different. The tendency to regress can itself come under stimulus control. A person may learn that in certain situations regression is rewarded.

The structural point of view which conceptualizes the complex ego functions and their relationships with id and superego processes is in accord with the view that aspects of external stimuli influence responses. What is necessary to observe this influence is a framework in which stimuli and responses are viewed flexibly. They can belong to complex classes, as do certain ego functions. These classes can compete with other classes, as in conflict. New classes can evolve or older classes can be mixed with newer ones, as in regressive movements. To identify the relevant classes of stimuli and responses, an understanding of the complexity of these internal processes is necessary. Once they are identified, their relationships can be studied.

STRUCTURAL DEFINITION OF RESPONSE AND STIMULUS CLASSES

Psychoanalytic theory, through its insights into the development of personality patterns, gives us important clues about the definition of these response and stimulus classes. Analytic findings direct our attention to the common denominators of various seemingly different behaviors. A child who is disruptive in school and who also shies away from his peers may be having difficulty with a single issue: dependency on adults. A broad behavioral class could be defined around this issue and the various ways the child obtains dependency gratification from adults in the form of attention. The types of stimuli provided by adults, in the context of our understanding of drive organization, would help us to distinguish which stimuli were important in influencing this broad response class.

Essentially, Freud's structural theory recognizes a functional compartmentalization of various processes. The id, ego, and superego each have certain characteristics which define them. In constructing a psychoanalytic formulation, we observe how derivatives and subfunctions of these structures combine to account for given symptoms, character traits, and behaviors.

If we view these structures as superordinate stimulus and response classes, we can define stimulus and response subclasses from them. This flexible conceptualization of structures and their derivatives as stimulus and response classes allows for a study in the present of how the spatial and temporal qualities of the environment influence the derivative response classes.

E. THE ADAPTIVE POINT OF VIEW

According to the adaptive point of view, behavior is determined by reality. The history of the concept of reality in psychoanalytic theory has already been discussed. Hartmann's (1939) contributions to the adaptive point of view emphasize that the organism, as a product of evolution, is adapted or potentially adapted to reality from birth. The ego apparatuses of primary autonomy are instruments which guarantee man's preparedness for an average expectable environment. Erikson (1956) takes Hartmann's concept one step further and sees man as potentially adapted not only to one average expectable environment but to a whole evolving series of such environments (Rapaport, 1959, pp. 57-63).

The concept of the ego as an instrument of adaptation fostered the development of many new concepts which have enabled us more fully to understand certain aspects of ego functioning. The concepts of primary autonomy, relative autonomy, neutralized energy, and mastery, and the re-examination of the development of the psychic structure, all highlight aspects of the relationships of the ego to reality as well as to other components of the psychic apparatus. In the present context, however, we need to examine these developments only in terms of their significance for the learning variables.

Implicit in the concept of neutralized energy, or structures which have neutralized energy at their disposal, is the relatively autonomous nature of this energy. Curiosity, interest, and exploration can be gratifying in themselves, and kept separate from sexual or aggressive drive gratification. It should be understood that neutralized structures exist in a hierarchy which basically may be related to the drives, and are therefore only relatively neutral. Those structures with predominantly neutralized energy tend to be more directly responsive to reality, however, than those structures which are predominantly energized by drive energies.

The adaptive point of view, like the dynamic, genetic, economic, and structural points of view, can contribute to the definition of response and stimulus classes. Definitions of these classes can be based on relatively autonomous ego activities. The response classes are defined by the ego functions: thinking, curiosity, explorativeness, interest, etc. The influencing stimuli are defined by what is experienced as gratifying in relation to their activity, such as problem-solving, accomplishment, newness, or mastery; functions which have both drive and neutralized energies are defined in a complex manner, as indicated in the discussion of structures. The response and stimulus classes will be defined according to a psychodynamic formulation which takes into account the relatively autonomous and drive aspects of the behaviors.

It might seem that Hartmann's (1939) contributions would pose a special problem for the hypothesis that aspects of environmental stimuli have a direct relationship to behavior. His consideration of "rational thinking," "means-end relationships," "synthetic function," and "adaptation" emphasizes a hierarchy of organizational principles which influence final behaviors. According to these concepts, the fully developed ego is not a slave to any one set of internal or external stimuli, but is regulated by principles of its own. Stimuli are processed through a complex series of channels which regulate, integrate, and synthesize them. Behavior is not the result of any one variable, but of the total process.

These conceptions, however, do not negate our hypothesis, for reasons I have already mentioned. To repeat what was said earlier, the complexity of ego functions and their relationships with the id and superego processes are in accord with the view that aspects of external stimuli influence responses. What is necessary to observe this influence is a framework in which stimuli and responses are viewed flexibly. They can belong to complex classes, as do certain ego functions. These classes can compete with other classes, as in conflict. New classes can evolve or older classes can be mixed with newer ones, as in regressive movements. To identify the relevant classes of stimuli and responses, an understanding of the complexity of these internal processes is necessary. Once they are identified, their relationships can be studied.

A special case exists when apparatuses of primary autonomy either do not develop, whether for maturational or functional reasons, or have developed but are secondarily involved in conflict and therefore do not function at full capacity. The person's discriminative abilities would be affected, which in turn would have implications for the manner in which the classes of stimuli and responses develop.

This is similar to the importance of intact apparatuses of primary autonomy in the proper development of structures. The integrity of the apparatuses of primary autonomy is necessary for structure formation, as well as for the formation of stimulus and response classes. Later experiences are responsible for the characteristics of these structures or classes.

4

TOWARD A LEARNING POINT
OF VIEW

Psychoanalytic theory has considered reality first in terms of the drives, then in terms of structures (particularly the ego structure), and finally in terms of adaptation. The adaptive point of view ascribes great importance to environmental forces. Even so, the environment's main effect is on certain internal processes, either as it influences the maturation of the organism, or as it evokes inborn preparedness or potentialities of the organism. In turn, these internal processes lead to change in behavior. Reality is still basically a subjective reality.

The next logical step in the development of psychoanalytic theory is a consideration of the area of learning theory which conceptualizes how external stimuli can, in independence of their subjective meanings, act as determinants of behavior. The conceptualization of external stimuli in operant learning theory—the learning variables—can be usefully incorporated into psychoanalytic theory provided that the learning variables meet certain criteria. The organismic point of view asserts that no behavior stands in isolation, that all behavior is part of the integral and indivisible personality. According to Rapaport (1959), this thesis demands that the explanation of any behavior fit into the theory of the functioning of the total personality. He says, "...an explanation of behavior, in order to have any claim of completeness, must specify its place within the functional and structural framework of the total personality and therefore must include statements about the degree and kind of involvement of the behavior in light of all the relevant conceptualized aspects of the personality" (p. 43).

Two criteria have been established for a learning model to be integrated into psychoanalytic theory. One, it must provide a way of looking at a behavior which will bring forth some new aspect or dimension of it. Two, it must be so conceptualized that it is functionally related to the other psychoanalytic points of view.

Both of these criteria have been met. A consideration of the objective properties of stimuli was shown to be an addition to current psychoanalytic theory. The preceding discussion has shown how stimuli and the responses they influence can be defined by each metapsychological viewpoint. The dynamic point of view identifies the relevant responses and the reinforcing and discriminative stimuli. The genetic point of view defines broad classes of stimuli and responses from a developmental perspective. The economic point of view emphasizes the efficacy of the stimulus classes, as well as the rigidity of the response classes. The structural point of view further defines the stimulus and response classes in terms of their broadness, their ingredients, and their relationships with each other. The adaptive point of view demonstrates how classes of stimuli and responses can be defined, not only by drives and structures, but by the interaction of the ego with the environment as well.

It has been shown how each metapsychological perspective can contribute to the definition of the learning variables, just as each of the analytic perspectives contributes to the definition of the others. The learning variables can therefore be conceptualized within the psychoanalytic framework. They are, on the one hand, distinct concepts which offer a distinct view of the multiple determination of behavior. They are, on the other hand, capable of sharing a common framework with the psychoanalytic perspectives. The criterion that each aspect of behavior be treated as part of an integrated whole has been met. It is therefore possible to formulate a new learning perspective.

We now have a method of looking at behaviors in the present in relationship to the stimuli which precede them and the stimuli which follow them. At the same time, we can conceptualize these behaviors and stimuli as belonging to broad classes which have dynamic, genetic, economic, structural, and adaptive aspects. A frame of reference has therefore been created which incorporates the contributions of operant learning theory within psychoanalytic theory:

1. Psychoanalysis can define the response and stimulus classes through its multiple perspectives.

2. Operant variables can afford additional insight into the interaction of these responses and stimuli in the present. The selectiveness of behavior, its frequency, modification, and resistance to change, may be more fully understood by taking these learning variables into account.

This psychoanalytic learning perspective can be conceptualized diagrammatically (Figure 2). The operant learning approach is designated by the horizontal direction of the interactive elements, the stimulus and response classes. These horizontal variables do not exist in isolation, but are connected to the development and current organization of the psychic apparatus, as indicated by the vertical direction. The intrapsychic factors represent the metapsychological points of view which are continually defining the structure and components of the classes of responses and stimuli. As can be observed, the classes of responses and stimuli exist in a developmental and dynamic continuum with the intrapsychic variables which define them. The bottom set of boxes, which represent current functioning, are drawn smaller to indicate that they are derived from earlier, broader, less differentiated classes of responses and stimuli.

In summary, for a complete behavioral analysis, the variables considered by both psychoanalytic and operant learning theories should be combined. Besides their different histories, methodologies, and terminologies, the difference between the two theories' views of behavior has been a primary reason for their staying apart.

To create a bridge between these two theories without compromising important principles of either, a model has here been presented in which the conception of broad, superordinate, stage-specific stimulus and response classes was shown to relate psychoanalytic concepts about the organization of a given personality with its environment. Stimuli and responses operating in the present were demonstrated to be related to the past history and organization of the personality via the evolution of stimulus and response classes throughout development. These classes—the very

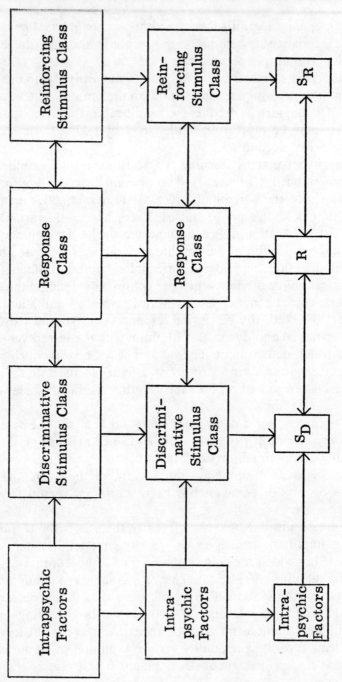

Figure 2. Vertical direction indicates development; horizontal direction indicates interactions at each phase.

basis of personality organization—are in constant interaction with the environmental forces, which have impact because of their association with these classes.

The development of a learning-theory model which incorporates psychodynamic notions about complex personality patterns allows psychoanalysis to define stimulus and response classes in terms of ingredients and development. Operant learning concepts can then be used in a uniform framework to show how these classes interact, both throughout development and in the present.

5

ILLUSTRATION OF THE LEARNING
POINT OF VIEW

In this chapter I will illustrate the psychoanalytic learning perspective with aspects of a clinical case, discuss the relative roles of the "inner" and "outer" control systems of behavior, and comment on considerations for intervention in the psychoanalytic situation and other settings. The goal of this chapter is illustration and further development of aspects of the learning perspective rather than documentation of its clinical usefulness. Usefulness was established at the level of theory, by demonstrating that the learning variables would add compatibly another dimension to the multiple approaches psychoanalysis uses to understand behavior. To focus on specific clinical usefulness would shift the level of conceptualization and emphasis.

A. Selected Aspects of a Clinical Example

A young man with predominantly oral personality traits suffered a reactive depression precipitated by the loss of an important relationship with a girl friend to whom he had had an ambivalent attachment. In reaction to the loss, he experienced an identification with the representation of the lost person, and directed his feelings of anger at his girl friend toward himself. This is a simplified but classic formulation of one kind of depression.

The young man's depression was of neurotic proportions. At first his family and friends displayed a good deal of warm concern and later began catering to him. His depression continued and his family and friends got rather fed up and decided to cut down on their catering. Finally, at the urging of his family and friends, the young man consulted a psychiatrist. At this time, family and friends gave him more regular attention and his depression lifted somewhat. Upon evaluation, the psychiatrist obtained an understanding of the dynamics, including the secondary-gain aspects of the attention the young man was receiving, and concluded that the patient had little psychotic potential but seemed highly manipulative and gratified in his regressed state. The family again began pressing the man to do more for himself, and only occasionally did anything for him. With therapy, he began to gain some understanding of his depression. Nevertheless his condition deteriorated and his symptoms became more resistant to change. With continued therapy, the psychiatrist believed that the patient was acquiring more understanding of his difficulties. Yet, though the secondary gain seemed nonexistent, his maladaptive behavior and symptoms stubbornly persisted.

The secondary gain can partially account for the initial persistence of the symptoms, but more needs to be understood about their fluctuation: They worsened and became more resistant to change each time the secondary gain was reduced. It could be hypothesized that the loss of some of the secondary gain was another experience of loss similar to that which precipitated the depression. In that case, attempts to reduce the secondary gain would reinforce the original depression. If the therapist accepts this explanation, he is damned if he does and damned if he doesn't. Gratification maintains the depression. Some lessening of gratification intensifies it.

The psychoanalytic learning perspective may add some insight to this not uncommon situation.

In order to apply the psychoanalytic learning perspective to this case, the learning variables must be defined by the contributions of each metapsychological perspective.[1] From the dynamic point of view, the relevant responses and influencing stimuli can be defined. The reinforcers can be defined as oral reinforcers from the oral drive organization. After the loss of his oral drive object, this patient identified with his lost object and directed his anger inward. There was a partial diffusion of the drive components of the oral organization and aspects of the aggressive drive were directed

---

[1]In practice, depending upon the case, one or another of the metapsychological perspectives may be more important in defining the relevant learning variables.

against the self. Reinforcers can be defined by the vicissitudes of the drives. There was self-directed anger. There was also a libidinized self-love. Most probably the man was gaining some oral-sadistic pleasure in draining his friends and family of their patience and energies, as well as gratifying his dependency needs by their attention. The reinforcers in this case can be listed: oral drive objects for libidinal needs (friends and family), oral drive objects for aggressive sadistic needs (friends and family), self-directed love (libidinal, self), self-directed anger (aggressive, self).

The first two require the presence of drive objects, which can be defined as discriminative stimuli; only in their presence will gratification take place. While the second two do not require the presence of drive objects, it is possible that drive objects—or, more likely, fantasies about them—served as discriminative stimuli. The responses are those which have as their consequence any one of the four types of gratification; they would be the oral-dependent draining responses and the depressive responses.

The genetic point of view highlights the development of these stimuli and responses in terms of broad classes related to particular developmental stages. Since we do not have a full clinical history of this case, little can be said about this point of view as it applies here. It can be postulated that the responses and stimuli given above are part of broad classes formed during the patient's oral stage of development and elaborated during later stages.

The structural point of view would emphasize the relationship between these classes and others. The ego's tendency toward identification with lost objects; the severity of the superego, which would not allow an experience of the rage associated with the loss; and the id's agression and hunger for dependency gratification are all aspects of this case which could be conceptualized by the structural hypothesis. These structures could be defined as response and stimulus classes, of which the more specific responses and stimuli causing this depression are members. There would be stimulus classes based on aggressive and dependent gratifications. There would be response classes based on aggressive and dependency-seeking behaviors, prohibitions against these, and taking in or identifying with lost objects. These various response and stimulus classes would interact to form new levels of organization resulting in response classes organized around depressive and dependency-seeking behaviors and stimulus classes centering on sadistic, erotic, and masochistic gratifications.

The intensity of certain kinds of object relations and coping styles and the relative paucity of others can be conceptualized in economic terms. There is relatively little energy attached to developmentally more advanced defenses and relationship styles which might offer alternatives to the early oral styles. The adaptive point of view can further highlight this in terms of the lack of neutralized energy available for relatively autonomous functions, or more generally for those functions that are important for adaptation to the environment. In learning-theory terms, the maladaptive response classes would be quite rigid and the stimuli influencing them would be quite efficacious. Other classes of responses and stimuli would be relatively inactive.

Now that the responses and stimuli have been defined and characterized, their role, which is independent of their subjective meanings, can be examined.

The depressive and dependent responses had as their consequence the various types of oral gratification described; because the reinforcers were of a number of types—i.e., oral object erotic and sadistic, masochistic, and autoerotic—some gratification would take place most of the time. The autoerotic and masochistic gratifications could take place even in the absence of objects. The object-erotic and sadistic gratifications might take place no matter what the object tried to do.

The depressive and dependency-seeking responses were described as being derived from other, more general, response classes; drive behaviors, prohibitions against them, and taking in or identifying behaviors. These symptomatic responses then would be quite a significant aspect of the behavioral repertory, having a substantial base in other response classes.

Furthermore, it was pointed out that the maladaptive responses were rigid and the stimuli which influenced them quite efficacious.

From these considerations alone, the persistence of the patient's illness is understandable. His symptoms were substantial and rigid and under the control of a number of potent reinforcers, one of which might be operating at any time.

It was noticed, however, that his symptoms fluctuated. To consider this phenomenon will require our focusing on the schedule of reinforcement, whatever its type. Understanding the effects of the schedule of reinforcement will add a new dimension to the concept of secondary gain. After a time, the secondary gain or reinforcement became more variable and intermittent. The drive objects—the family and friends—partially withdrew their availability as reinforcers. As a result, the depressive and dependency responses increased and became more resistant to change.

Later, with more continuous reinforcement, the frequency of the symptoms lessened. The schedule had been changed to a more continuous one. Interestingly, an increase in the secondary gain made the symptoms less resistant. With psychotherapy and another decrease in the secondary gain, the symptoms again became more frequent and more resistant. Despite the patient's heightened insight and the virtual nonexistence of secondary gain, the symptoms not only persisted but worsened. Let us assume that the patient's insights were sound and that he and the psychiatrist had a good working relationship. The above phenomenon can be accounted for by considering the effects of different reinforcement schedules. When a schedule of reinforcement changes slowly from a nearly continuous one to a highly unpredictable, variable one, the behavior under the control of this schedule will persist. Surprisingly, the highly variable schedule, in which there is only occasional reinforcement, will maintain behavior in a more persistent and stubborn fashion than the continuous one. If the schedule were a variable ratio one, the frequency of the behavior might be high. If the schedule were a variable interval schedule with particularly long intervals, the behavior would be most resistant to change. While at home with his family, or visiting with close friends, the patient was in the presence of the discriminative stimuli, the stimuli that had in the past set the occasion for the reinforcement. These people had to respond gratifyingly only infrequently and inadvertently to maintain the patient's maladaptive functioning. A variable interval schedule could become so variable that it would indeed seem nonexistent. This rare, inadvertent reinforcement can therefore maintain behavior so stubbornly that it could offset the gains from the patient's new insight.

In reality the situation is even more complex, since the patient's fantasies, thoughts, or experiences of certain affects could also serve as discriminative stimuli. As these might often occur in interpersonal situations, some additional inadvertent reinforcement might be obtained. The more variable and infrequent the reinforcement, the more resistant to change the symptoms would become.

Self-directed love and self-directed anger and their accompanying thoughts, affects, and fantasies were also experienced by the patient as reinforcing. Since they were under the patient's control, they were probably nearly continuous, and therefore would not be as resistant to change as the phenomenon just considered. These internal experiences could be dealt with in psychotherapy.

The learning perspective shows how the reinforcers in the environment—in this case, the way family and friends responded to his symptoms—are important determinants of aspects of the patient's behavior. It is possible to hypothesize that he became angry or further depressed when the frequency of reinforcement or secondary gain was decreased. If this is true it should account for only a temporary worsening of symptoms. If the ego structure is basically intact and the secondary gain is not maintained, symptoms should improve. The learning perspective is particularly valuable because it offers a specific explanation for the increased resistance of the symptoms, based on experimental evidence of the effects of changing the schedule of reinforcement. This could be tested by altering the schedule to see if the responses changed in a predictable fashion.

It was mentioned that the patient's family and friends as well as his fantasies served as discriminative stimuli for his maladaptive responses. The maladaptive behaviors were likely to occur more often when these stimuli were present than when they were absent. Recognizing the discriminative stimuli increases our understanding of all the determinants of the maladaptive behavior.

A specific aspect of the way discriminative stimuli influenced this patient's behavior still further explains why his maladaptive responses increased after therapy began. Beyond initial history-taking and basic interest, the therapist, aware of the influence of secondary gain in maintaining this patient's symptoms, was careful to follow the abstinence principle and not gratify the patient's use of symptoms. The selective nonreinforcement in the therapy setting coupled with the reinforcement occurring outside of therapy, however, provided the ingredients for the phenomenon of behavioral contrast. As mentioned earlier (pp. 9-10), if behavior which is under the control of a number of discriminative stimuli undergoes extinction in some settings, in other settings where reinforcement is maintained the behavior will correspondingly increase.

For a full explanation of this patient's illness, it is necessary to understand him from all perspectives. The dynamic perspective focuses on the object loss and the anger that was turned inward, as well as the libidinal and aggressive aspects of his relationships. Genetically, his oral personality characteristics predisposed him to this reaction. Economically, the amount of energy fixated at oral levels rather than at more advanced levels, and the lack of neutralized energy available to use for adaptive functioning, compromised his response flexibility. Structurally, his punitive superego fostered the ego's inability to tolerate the id's object hunger. The resultant anger fostered an identification with, and a turning against, the lost object. Adaptively, there was a loss of relatively autonomous functions, in this case the ability to cope with the environment, as a consequence of involvement in the depression.

These perspectives, which formulate the patient's intrapsychic functions, explain most of his depressive reaction. In addition, however, they help us to define certain learning variables which allow psychoanalytic theory to make use of another perspective: the learning perspective. The learning perspective contributed to the conceptualization of this case beyond what was possible with the usual psychoanalytic perspectives alone. The psychoanalytic model alone could not take into account the full influence of the reinforcing or discriminative variables. Without the learning perspective, the explanation of the changing frequency and resistance to change of the depressive symptoms would probably have been based predominantly on intrapsychic variables such as the therapist's making incorrect, inappropriately timed, too deep interpretations, or his ignoring the patient's use of the defense of displacement. While these factors may be operative in many cases, they should not obscure the significance of still other variables which may influence behavior. It was shown that the pattern and schedule of reinforcement had a determining effect on behavior that was independent of its subjective meaning. As the schedule of reinforcement became more variable and intermittent (the secondary gain lessened), the maladaptive behavior became more frequent and more resistant to change. As the schedule became more continuous (the secondary gain increased), the behavior became less frequent and less resistant to change. These observations are in accord with the experimental findings of operant learning outlined earlier.

The discriminative stimuli influenced the maladaptive behavior by setting the occasion for their reinforcement. The maladaptive responses occurred with higher frequency in those situations, around family and friends and in the context of certain fantasies, which in the past set the occasion for their reinforcement. In addition, it was observed that after the patient became involved in therapy, another aspect of the influence of discriminative stimuli on his behavior resulted in an increase in his maladaptive responses. This was the phenomenon of behavioral contrast.

The learning perspective first focuses our attention on the environmental consequences of maladaptive responses. It then focuses our attention on the schedule or patterning of these consequences. Finally, it helps us attend to the effect of discriminative stimuli on these responses, including the striking phenomenon of behavioral contrast. The learning perspective could not have been applied to this case, however, without first understanding the case from the other points of view. The other points of view, which account for many of the determinants of the depression, also define the learning variables. This makes it possible to identify them and consequently to understand their operation in natural settings.

B. Relative Roles of Inner and Outer Control Systems

A major tenet of psychoanalytic theory is that there is a progressive internalization of the factors that determine behavior. In this sense, psychoanalysis focuses on an inner control system. For example, in treating an adult, the therapist tends to study how the patient may distort his perceptions and/or set up his environment to reinforce or support his behavior. While in the clinical case just discussed the development and organization of the personality determined what functioned as discriminative and reinforcing stimuli and in this sense the stimuli were defined in terms of their unique meaning to a given person, the schedule or pattern of these stimuli operated in part independently of the patient and had an equally important determining effect on his behavior. In assessing the many determinants of behavior, one must come to grips both with the degree to which the patient distorts and/or sets up his environment to reinforce his behavior and the degree to which the environment independently determines his behavior. What are the relationships between the inner and outer control systems? In the case cited, the role of the outer control system was emphasized to demonstrate its influence on behavior. In any given case, however, the role of the outer control system may range from minimal importance to major importance, depending upon the organization of the patient's personality and the organization of his immediate environment. Consider the following examples:

A person with a rigid, repetitive personality pattern might be able to respond with only a few general, unselective patterns. In terms of stimulus and response classes, this person has only a few general response classes to deal with a variety of inner and outer stimuli. The rigid obsessional who responds to most situations with classic obsessional patterns—ruminating, doubting, intellectualizing, or delaying—would be a good example of this kind of personality. Since this person uses only a few general response classes, in most situations he is to a large degree impervious to variations in his environment. His patterns are so repetitive, encompassing, and limited that there is little else but these patterns to be reinforced. Since there is no competing behavior, the relative effect of the stimulus control of his behavior might be minimal. As a side note, behavioral therapists rarely take into account the fact that the behaviors they reinforce may be only other members of a class of maladaptive responses (e.g., substituting one obsessional defense for another). The general point to be made is that when the behavioral repertory has little flexibility and variety, the outer control system may exert only a minimal effect.

To illustrate the other extreme: Another patient is oversensitive to environmental cues. He appears to have little inner control over his behavior. He behaves according to the presence or absence of a drive object and takes his cues, so to speak, from the drive object when it is present. His personality is uneven in that patterns from all levels of development may be activated, depending upon the cues in his immediate environment. Some hysteroid or borderline personalities show this characteristic. The therapist's goal with such a person might be to help him internalize control. At any given moment, however, the behavior he is emitting may be largely determined by the contingencies and schedules of reinforcement in his environment.

These two examples show how personality organization may determine the relative importance of the person's inner and outer control systems. The organization of his environment may play a similar role. If his environment is organized to regularly reinforce only certain behavior, its effect on him will be quite powerful. For example, if the person in the second illustration were in a situation in which drive gratification was dependent on only a few ways of behaving, these behaviors would dramatically increase in frequency. If, on the other hand, the environment were disorganized and reinforcement capricious, his behavior would be predominantly influenced by his inner control system.

Of course, a person might respond to the environmental organization or disorganization as his cue. In that case it could be assumed that these more global percepts of the environment, rather than the more specific patterns of reinforcement, would affect his responses. This analysis makes no a priori assumptions about what types or aspects of stimuli any given person will attend to or experience as reinforcing. Environmental organization or disorganization could certainly be conceptualized as providing stimuli related to either pleasurable or aversive experiences, and thus operate as positively or negatively reinforcing.

Obviously, most people and most environments are not organized at the extremes presented in these examples. While some people have an uncanny skill in finding environments which support their characterological patterns, in studying any particular person it is important to analyze all the determinants of his behavior and attempt to assess their relative effects.

C. CONSIDERATIONS FOR INTERVENTIONS

1. THE PSYCHOANALYTIC SITUATION

The example of a case of depression illustrated how a psychoanalytic learning perspective can facilitate the conceptualization of the many variables affecting a patient's behavior at any particular time. It demonstrated how the configuration of external reality in terms of the contingencies of reinforcement, the schedules of reinforcement, and the discriminative stimulus control, when defined psychoanalytically, can interact with intrapsychic determinants more fully to explain a patient's behavior. It was also demonstrated how both internal and external systems play an important role in determining a given behavioral pattern, and in addition how the relationships between the internal and external systems depend on both the configuration of the patient's personality and his environment.

The psychoanalytic situation is unique. It is an environment with its own design which is optimally used for patients with certain personality organizations. In the psychoanalytic situation the tendency is to focus on the patient's internal system. One way to view the psychoanalytic situation is to define it as a process with circumscribed boundaries. This process comprises the relationship between the analyst and his patient within which patterns can be explored from the point of view of the patient's internal system so that the patient can observe his inner life. Through the development of the transference in this setting, the patient can explore the reality he creates. To the degree that the patient can explore his inner life and at the same time develop a transference to explore the reality he creates, his external system becomes a focus of the analysis, mainly in terms of its relationship to the processes set up in the analytic situation.

To what degree the analytic situation itself becomes the major focus depends, of course, on certain of the patient's ego capacities, which differ among different patients. This is especially true since the scope of analytic treatment has expanded to include patients whose ego structures may not permit them to develop a relatively organized transference neurosis and where the boundary between the transference, external reality, and the reality of the analytic situation may not be clearly demarcated. The psychoanalytic learning perspective within the context of the traditional psychoanalytic points of view provides a model in which one can begin to conceptualize the complex interrelationships between the internal and external systems.

However, a consideration of how to use the increased conceptual capability of this model leads to many difficult issues. A most basic issue concerns the misuse of new understanding as a rationalization for generating poorly thought out changes in technique. Because of their relatively explicit formulation, their relationship to experimental data, and their apparent ease of implementation, behavioral principles have considerable appeal for use in developing interventions. In formulating a psychoanalytic learning approach, the goal has been to open psychoanalysis to the contributions from learning theories and to delineate the complex relationships between the variables conceptualized by learning theories and the variables conceptualized by psychoanalytic theory. The model presented here offers a broad conceptual framework in which the variables studied by each discipline can be seen as interacting, so that interventions derived from learning principles can be studied in the context of their implications for each psychoanalytic metapsychological point of view. In considering implementation of an intervention derived from a psychoanalytic learning perspective, it becomes especially important to explore the potential intervention in the context of its dynamic, genetic, structural, and economic implications, and empirically assess it in the analytic situation.

For example, it might be reasoned that parameters could be systematically constructed from reinforcement principles. The traditional use of parameters in the treatment of phobias might be reviewed in this context. If a specific technique is developed it should be conceptualized in the context of its potential effect or interference in the natural evolution of the transference in terms of developmental level, the interplay of dynamic forces operating on it, and the economics of its final crystallization. In this way the parameter constructed for an initial purpose would be developed with due consideration for the context in which it could be analyzed later for an optimal analytic result.

What is being emphasized is that a psychoanalytic learning perspective, which suggests the use of many learning techniques, should not be misused as a basis for unsystematic and ill-judged therapeutic experimentation. Any suggestions for technical changes must be considered from the perspective of all the metapsychological viewpoints and in terms of how they would affect the optimal analytic goal of structural personality change.

Even with this caution in mind, a focus on specific technical considerations should emerge only after additions to psychoanalytic theory have been explored in terms of their theoretical consistency, their capacity to highlight or generate new ideas, and their use in opening the door to contributions from other disciplines.

However, some areas of the analytic process in which the learning perspective may enhance the conceptualization of complex phenomena should be mentioned. The following questions will illustrate some of these areas.

1. Could the concepts of differential reinforcement, discriminative learning, and discriminatory capacity enhance understanding of the development of the working alliance and observing ego, transference, and the capacity to transform character pathology into symptoms (ego syntonic into ego dystonic)? For example, could these concepts improve understanding of the *new learning* which occurs in the analytic process which results in the capacity to discriminate subtle emotional states, perceive preconscious wishes, and perceive new transference states while still maintaining an effective balance between an observing and experiencing ego?

2. Could the concepts of stimulus and response generalization help to conceptualize aspects of situations in which the structure of a transference does not develop into a fully organized transference neurosis but retains an undifferentiated character?

3. Could the concepts of stimulus and response generalization also enhance understanding of aspects of difficulties in the working-through process, where an apparent transference resolution followed by derepression and some apparent working through does not lead to a generalization of the patient's apparent growth into other areas of his life?

4. Could the concepts of a deprivation and satiation operation aid in understanding regressive transference phenomena which occur in relationship to the analyst's neutrality and relative abstinence?

5. Could the concept of extinction aid in understanding some issues in working through that relate to ego processes involved in the final relinquishment of maladaptive behaviors, symptoms, and character traits after the nuclear conflicts underlying them have been analyzed and worked through? For example, would different patients demonstrate different resistance to and patterns of relinquishment (e.g., slow and steady or in bursts) which would correspond to different known extinction curves and would in part be related to patterns of gratification in early life, life outside of the analysis, or the analysis itself? Could this help in understanding aspects of mourning?

6. Could the concepts of generalization and behavioral contrast aid in understanding the phenomenon of acting out? For example, under optimal conditions a patient discriminates the analytic situation from settings outside the analysis. Yet at times it is in his interest to generalize the results of analytic understanding

into other areas of his life. As described earlier, behavioral contrast occurs when behaviors which are occurring in two situations increase in frequency in one, while undergoing extinction in the other. The two settings are clearly discriminated so that instead of the extinction generalizing, behavioral contrast occurs. From an observational standpoint, this is similar to the phenomenon of acting out. In one sense acting out might usefully be viewed as an overdiscrimination between the analytic setting and other settings coupled with a limitation of discriminated generalizations. An interesting speculation that emerges from this conceptual framework is: In working with a patient with the tendencies described above, could rigorous abstinence inadvertently set up a situation more favorable to acting out than less rigorous abstinence? In the rigorous abstinence position, extinction occurs more sharply in the analytic setting than in other settings. For the patient who already overdiscriminates and therefore has a tendency toward acting out, rigorous abstinence could conceivably facilitate his overdiscrimination and therefore his acting out. Could this conceptualization aid in focusing attention on the specific ego functions that need to be explored in such patients as well as on issues in the construction of an optimal analytic treatment setting?

7. Could the concept of reinforcement and its focus on the consequences of an element of behavior, and the concept of a schedule of reinforcement, aid in understanding the competing effects of the outside environment in relationship to the patient's capacity to relinquish certain behavioral patterns and permit psychological growth to occur? For example, could these concepts encourage us to pay attention to how the outside environment may be systematically reinforcing certain of the patient's maladaptive patterns? The outside environment may be differentially reinforcing the patient's maladaptive patterns at the expense of his more adaptive ones.

8. In this context, could the concept of the schedule of reinforcement help to focus attention on an aspect of external reinforcement which might ordinarily go unnoticed? For example, it is known from learning experiments that extremely variable schedules of reinforcement can maintain behavior in a highly resistant and stubborn fashion. Such a schedule of reinforcement may be operative outside the analytic situation, without its being apparent to the patient or the analyst. Ironically, such variable schedules may more effectively compete with certain analytic goals than external rein-

forcement which is obvious to both the patient and the analyst and which they can understand and work with.

9. Could the concept of reinforcement and its emphasis on the consequences of behavior help us to understand aspects of the analyst's role in the analytic process? For example, could it be useful to conceptualize the analyst, in addition to the many ways he is already conceptualized, as a potential reinforcer (positive or negative) at different levels of development and with different valence and meaning, depending on the dynamic, genetic, and economic aspects of the transference at any particular time?

10. Along this same line of thought, could it enhance conceptual understanding of the analytic process to view the analyst's responses in terms of their schedule, in addition to their role in facilitating the associative work through clarifications and interpretations? Could viewing his responses in terms of a schedule yield further insight into the rate, configuration, and resistance to change in symptoms, behaviors, and character traits? For example, let us assume a situation in which an analyst usually maintains the abstinence position. Occasionally, however, while in a positive transference configuration with the patient, he yields to the patient's manipulations and gratifies him. In these circumstances, might it be found that this analyst later has a harder time analyzing these transference gratifications than would the analyst who offers gratification more regularly? Reinforcement theory tells us that variable schedules of reinforcement make behavior more resistant to change than do relatively continuous schedules.

11. Could findings from learning theory regarding the differential effects of different reinforcement schedules aid in understanding how optimally to construct parameters? For example, could it help in formulating a method to construct parameters relatively easy to analyze later in the analysis rather than parameters whose effects would be quite resistant to later analytic understanding?

These are only some of the possibilities that the learning perspective may offer for enhancing understanding of complex issues in the analytic situation. Obviously this subject requires a detailed systematic exploration, an exploration that would take us into the practical aspects of psychoanalysis and divert us from the main purpose of this monograph, which is to create a theoretical frame of reference. A consideration of these issues, however, does offer an opportunity for a wide range of thought and discussion.

2. OTHER SETTINGS

In situations where the external environment may exert significant influence, as in a therapeutic milieu, an educational setting,
or supportive psychotherapy, a psychoanalytic learning perspective can make a special contribution. It provides a framework for
a fairly explicit formulation of how environmental variables may
influence behavior.

This framework was illustrated with the case of depression
where it was demonstrated that when these variables are given
psychoanalytic meaning, they can be quite complex and their
identification in natural settings quite difficult. It was shown that
the reinforcers can be of many different types, some not at all obvious and their schedule or pattern so variable as to be almost
imperceptible. In addition, it was shown that the situations which
serve as discriminative stimuli can be specific or general and the
contingency operations involved in differential reinforcement and
discriminative learning can lead to either a generalization of responses or behavioral contrast.

Here I will focus on some principles of how to use this framework. The first use is to clarify or interpret to a person the functional relationships between his maladaptive behaviors and the
environmental variables influencing them. To the degree that behavior is influenced by environmental events which are not apparent to the person, such as a highly variable schedule, the
recognition of functional relationships between behavior and its
reinforcement may serve as a basis for a growing observing ego,
particularly in its function of recognition and anticipation. A person may be able to anticipate a situation in which his maladaptive
behavior is likely to occur, and anticipate and identify formerly
covert reinforcements.

In some situations the recognition of a functional relationship
may lead to a change in the meaning of a reinforcer, and as a
result that stimulus may become less reinforcing or nonreinforc-
ing. For example, a child who was reinforced with subtle attention
for misbehaving in class was told that one of the reasons he might
be having such a hard time controlling his conduct was that he
often got some attention after misbehaving, attention he seemed
to enjoy. To the degree that this child wished to increase his
adaptive capacities, he realized that gaining attention by misbe-
havior conflicted with his long-term goals. The identification of

the functional relationship brought the pleasure of the attention into conflict, thus changing its meaning. Attention became less reinforcing, and attention-getting behavior decreased.

A change of meaning may break a functional link between a behavior and its former reinforcer.

In persons with particularly strong ego capacities, the explicit formulation of a functional relationship between a maladaptive behavior and an unrecognized reinforcer may completely change the meaning of the reinforcer. For example, a man who constantly makes a fool of himself at business meetings because this behavior is intermittently followed by a flirtatious glance from an attractive secretary, may, upon recognizing the consequences (the flirtatious glances) which have been contributing to the maintenance of his behavior, come to experience her glance as manipulative instead of pleasurable.

Of course, with the child who misbehaves to get attention and the man who behaves foolishly for a flirtatious glance, it is most important to analyze the internal systems that maintain the tendencies to enact these behaviors and to experience these external reactions as reinforcing.

The recognition of functional relationships, however, will not compromise a long-range goal of general personality growth. On the contrary, the perceptive recognition of the external system may help a patient to focus on his internal system because of increased capacity to anticipate and observe his tendencies in relationship to external stimuli. Making such functional relationships explicit is part of every dynamic therapist's daily work. However, as mentioned earlier, the psychoanalytic learning model adds considerably to the appreciation of the many complex and subtle ways in which external stimuli can influence behavior.

A second and more obvious way in which a psychoanalytic learning analysis of an environmental configuration can be used is to make the members of that environment, such as the staff of a therapeutic milieu, aware of how they may be supporting a patient's maladaptive behavior. For example, in a residential treatment setting, five reinforcers related to diffusely organized libidinal and aggressive derivatives of oral, anal, and phallic drive organizations were identified in an eight-year-old child. We were able to list these reinforcers tentatively as generalized attention; masochism (self-pain); sadism (pain to others, either physical or psychological); the disruption of his environment; and exhibitionism. We could have broken down our list further to specify which levels of development—oral and anal—contributed to the masochism and sadism, but since he did not appear to discriminate that well internally it was not important for us to do so either. There were some indications of ego splitting, with repetitive response patterns involving apparently cooperative and even obsequious behavior, and sadistic, self-destructive, and provocative behavior. Many different situations seemed to serve as discriminative stimuli for this behavior. Without the staff's full awareness, reinforcement from them appeared to be contingent on the boy's many maladaptive behavioral patterns. The schedules of reinforcement ranged from relatively continuous for some of his behaviors to quite variable for others.

His maladaptive behaviors were so numerous, the discriminative stimulus control so general, the types of reinforcers so varied and potent, that the staff could hardly react to him without inadvertently reinforcing some component of his maladaptive patterns. It should be noted that we were aware of the intense ambivalence and uneven development that made these patterns necessary. We were further aware that, from one perspective, these patterns kept him involved in object relationships and maintained an internal organization, fragile though it was.

Nevertheless, the boy showed some capacity for warmth and sadness in his individual therapy sessions and was making progress there, although his situation was deteriorating in the school and residence. With varying degrees of awareness, the staff in the school and residence felt helpless, angry, and guilty about his failure to respond to treatment.

Attempts to discuss the staff's feelings with them and to understand the child's behavior as reflected by his internal system in terms of his ego structure, transference, acting out, or displacement, or the staff's countertransference, were not useful. What did prove useful was the specific delineation, from the psychoanalytic learning model, of his many specific patterns of dynamically identified maladaptive behaviors, the many specific events he experienced as reinforcing, the numerous situations which served as discriminative stimuli for the behaviors, and the many specific methods and schedules with which the staff was overtly or covertly reinforcing these maladaptive patterns.

This delineation provided the staff with some understanding of the complexity of the external variables. They could begin to observe the functional relationships between the external variables and behavior. This in turn helped them deal with their anxiety, and enhanced their observing egos. Instead of being caught up in their anxiety and defenses against helplessness, anger, and guilt, they were able to anticipate, delay, and respond to the boy in a flexible, adaptive manner. They became especially alert to the interaction patterns which supported his maladaptive behavior and were therefore able to relate to him in new ways. Aspects of this understanding of how he and his environment were involved in complex patterns which maintained his maladaptive behavior were communicated to the boy by the staff and his therapist. This helped him to anticipate and explore his tendencies as well as to bring the pleasure associated with some of his former reinforcers into conflict with his recognition of his long-range goals.

In a sense, this process of pointing out to the staff the complex ways in which they react to a child's behavior is similar to making the preconscious conscious in a patient in therapy. In this situation, however, what is brought to the staff's consciousness is not merely covert or preconscious wishes, but unattended to and, in this sense, preconscious aspects of their roles as environmental variables. While countertransference repression is certainly involved in this inattention, *an important aspect of it is the lack of a cognitive structure which would direct attention to the complexities of the environment.*

A crucial, yet simple, technique that emerged from staff discussions about this boy was to intervene with him before rather than as a consequence of his maladaptive patterns. The intervention often took the form of pointing out to him what he was signaling he was about to do and what effect he wanted to elicit from the environment. This approach helped him with his own anticipatory functions and provided reinforcement before rather than as a consequence of maladaptive behavior. As mentioned, his reinforcers were so varied that almost any reaction from the environment after a maladaptive behavior was reinforcing. In the anticipatory intervention, reflection and anticipation were reinforced. Moreover, because the staff's intervention was anticipatory, when it failed they were able to be firmer and less ambivalent in their limit-setting, minimizing reinforcement in this regard. As a consequence, they were better able to engage this boy in his more adaptive behavior that slowly emerged. His condition significantly improved over a six-month period.

While anticipatory intervention is in accord with psychodynamic reasoning, in this case it was derived from the learning model because this model focused explicitly on the timing of the external variables in relationship to behavior. The psychoanalytic model focused on this patient's ego structure, acting out, transferences, and displacements. It also focused on secondary gain and the special meanings of the boy's relationships with certain staff members, but it could not focus explicitly on certain complexities of the environment, a focus which was necessary for understanding all the determinants of the boy's behavior.

In this case the psychoanalytic learning analysis generated much new understanding but suggested only a relatively simple technique. Within behavioral theory there are many specific learning techniques, involving the systematic reinforcement of adaptive behavior and careful nonreinforcement or mild punishment of nonadaptive behavior, which can be used once the learning variables have been fully identified by a psychoanalytic learning perspective. However, these specific techniques may interfere with the general orientation of some milieus because they may detract from spontaneous affective components of relationships which are difficult to label but are essential to emotional growth. It is for this reason that specific techniques are minimized and stress is laid on the increased understanding which can enhance the therapeutic capacity of a staff without interfering with its spontaneity and autonomy. Often, merely alerting a staff to the ways in which they, as environmental variables, influence the patient's behavior increases their adaptational work capacities and makes specific behavioral programs unnecessary.

Certain conditions especially require the use of a psychoanalytic learning perspective. Pathological configurations, which reflect ego defects, incomplete structures, and early pregenital drive organizations, leave the regulation of behavior to a fragile and complex interaction between a disorganized internal system and a uniquely multipotent external system. The external system derives its potency partly from a drive organization which makes a wide variety of external configurations reinforcing. Without an adequate model to study the complex effects of external influence, there may be considerable difficulty in treating such persons because of their vulnerability to environmental influence.

Some adolescent patients with some of the above-mentioned characteristics may find intolerable an approach which focuses on their feelings. They may, however, be able to use an approach which brings to their attention how they and the environment interact to maintain certain maladaptive patterns. This approach might dovetail with the state of their ego structures at the beginning of treatment, when such patients often view the environment as the source of their problems. This approach may enhance their observing egos and awaken curiosity about their contributions to these patterns, which in turn may lead to the exploration of their internal systems.

Certain patients, such as those with addiction problems, have a unique capacity for repetitive, manipulative, maladaptive patterns. For these patients, who have defeated more than one therapeutic team, a psychoanalytic understanding of the many ways in which environmental configurations may support their behavior is essential. It may generate not only additional understanding but new treatment approaches based on dynamic and behavioral principles which can interrupt the stubborn maintenance of maladaptive patterns in these patients, so that they may leave themselves open for therapeutic relationships which will lead to long-range psychological growth.

Interestingly, these observations lead to some comments on education. In educational approaches, it is especially important to be able to conceptualize, within a model that appreciates emotional development, the aspects of the environment which contribute to learning.

Current interest in early child care means working with children at a time when the boundary between primary- and secondary-process thinking is indistinct and structure formation is incomplete. At this period of development, any interaction with the environment, whether its goals are social learning, cognitive stimulation, or behavior change, will have a major impact on emotional growth. Experiences with the environment will not only influence behavior in an immediate sense but, in interaction with maturation, lead to structure formation: the progressive internalization and stabilization of behavioral patterns. While object-relations theory has contributed much to our understanding of these complex relationships, the explicit formulation a psychoanalytic learning perspective can give a certain environmental variable may further enhance our conceptual capacity in this area.

The next chapter will illustrate this point through a consideration of one learning variable.

6

SOME THEORETICAL IMPLICATIONS OF A PSYCHOANALYTIC LEARNING PERSPECTIVE

How processes turn into structures is still an unsolved problem for psychoanalytic theory (Rapaport, 1959, p. 35). How do structures attain their characteristics?

In this chapter I will show how some of the learning variables can generate hypotheses about this question. While these hypotheses will not completely explain the phenomenon of structuralization, they will illustrate how the learning variables can further expand our understanding of important areas in psychoanalytic theory.

A. THE CONCEPT OF THE SCHEDULE OF REINFORCEMENT AND ITS IMPLICATIONS FOR STRUCTURE FORMATION

The factors which determine structure formation are most complex. An important one is the balance between frustration and gratification (Hartmann, Kris, and Loewenstein, 1946). There is no specific way to classify this balance, however. What are the implications of the varying degrees of this balance for the subsequent characteristics of the structure? Rapaport (1959) said that an important characteristic of a structure is its slow rate of change. "Structural determiners differ from motivational determiners in that they are relatively permanent; their rate of change is relatively slow" (p. 56).

What determines the permanence or rate of change of a structure? Are all structures the same in this respect, or do they differ according to the circumstances leading to their formation?

84

Learning experiments have shown that if the total amount of reinforcement, over a time period, is the same for two organisms but the schedule of reinforcement is different, the characteristics of the behavioral patterns formed as a consequence will be different (Ferster and Skinner, 1957). The pattern of gratification, therefore, is as important as its quantity. This fact has been confirmed by many psychoanalytic observers (Escalona, 1963; Mahler, 1963; Ritvo and Solnit, 1958). The pattern of gratification can, however, be quite intricate. Constructs which could focus on this pattern would add new levels of explanation.

The schedule of reinforcement is the schedule of rewards or gratifications which occur in relationship to a behavior or class of behaviors. Because the schedule of reinforcement has a lawful relationship to aspects of the behavior it influences, it is a useful construct to enhance our understanding of the relationship between patterns of gratification and frustration and behavior. It should be mentioned that other components of the experience of gratification besides its pattern, such as its affective quality, consistency, and depth, are not intentionally ignored or relegated to positions of unimportance. The schedule of reinforcement is presented as a framework within which to understand only one component of the gratification experience.

Different schedules of reinforcement have been described above (p. 11). Each schedule influences the behavior it is reinforcing in its own characteristic manner. One aspect of the schedule of reinforcement which is quite different for different schedules is the extinction time. For example, behavior which is reinforced on a continuous schedule will decrease in frequency rather quickly if reinforcement ceases. In contrast, a behavior which is reinforced on a variable interval schedule with long intervals may continue for a relatively long time after reinforcement ceases. The pattern of extinction, too, differs for different schedules. With some schedules the frequency of behavior declines smoothly and slowly, while with others it may decline in abrupt bursts. The pattern of behavior, while the behavior is maintained, is also affected by the type of reinforcement schedule: Some schedules maintain behavior at relatively low rates, others at relatively high rates.

The following discussion will show how the schedule of reinforcement could influence a structure's stability—that is, its rate of change. It will also show how the schedule of reinforcement could influence the characteristics a structure exhibits during functioning and the characteristics it exhibits while changing.

Before examining these relationships, the more general relationships between a reinforcement schedule and a structure should be examined.

Earlier, it was stated that an internal structure could be conceptualized in learning terms as a superordinate response class, that is, a group of responses or functions that are interrelated and have a common goal. Structures or superordinate response classes are broad in their influence, affecting many different subsidiary responses or functions. Their slow rate of change is an important characteristic: If a group of functions changed too quickly, it might not warrant being defined as a structure. What is not clear is how stable a group of functions has to be to merit that definition. What is usually meant by a stable or slowly changing group of functions is that they will operate without internal or external support for fairly extended periods of time. In the short run, they are not dependent on internal or external stimulation. Different structures in different people, however, may vary in the amount of stimulation required to maintain them.

One dimension of a series of functions attaining the degree of stability necessary to be considered a structure can be conceptualized in the following manner.

Initially the infant responds directly to internal or external stimulation. There is no delay between stimulus and response, and no capacity for functions to operate in independence of stimulation. The mother tries to respond to his needs on a relatively continuous schedule, thus helping him organize his functions. With the maturation of the central nervous system, the capacity to delay evolves. To encourage the development of this capacity, the mother must allow delay and frustration to occur. As a result, gratification becomes less continuous—more variable and intermittent. The new variable schedule maintains the infant's capacity to function for short periods of time without stimulation. At some later time a group of functions becomes sufficiently organized and stable to be considered a structure. For example, the internal representation of the object may become constant enough in the third year of life to be considered structuralized.

To permit maintenance of functioning without external stimulation, the schedule of reinforcement must become variable in accord with maturation. As was indicated earlier, many variable schedules will maintain functioning with only occasional reinforcement. An aspect of structuralization in learning terms, then, would be a function maintained on a variable schedule. The function operates for periods of time without continuous reinforcement.

In summary, what in the psychoanalytic conceptualization is internalization and structure formation may be viewed operationally as a pattern which in the short run is not dependent on external stimulation. It appears to be under the influence of an internal organization. The learning-theory counterpart is a pattern maintained on an intermittent schedule of stimulation, where the stimulation is so infrequent that the pattern appears not to depend on it. An argument over whether a pattern is really regulated from inside or outside should not cloud a more important issue. From an operational viewpoint, learning theory and psychoanalysis have described similar observed phenomena, focused on different components of them, and then described those different components in different theoretical constructs. The purpose of this discussion is only to see if the components observed and constructs used by learning theory can, in the context of a psychoanalytic learning perspective, enhance our understanding of these phenomena. In the following discussion the concepts of response class and reinforcement schedule will be used with the assumption that the response classes are under schedules sufficiently variable for the response classes to be relatively stable.

We will first focus on the implications of the reinforcement schedule for the stability of a structure. Here the relevant aspect of the reinforcement schedule is its particular extinction pattern. This will be illustrated by two examples of simple schedules of reinforcement. The inferences one may make from these simple schedules are intuitive and are similar to conclusions drawn from infant observations and reconstructive work. Later it will be shown how a consideration of these same variables can lead to new hypotheses.

It should be pointed out that the term gratification is used here in an operational context. Gratification as reinforcement is defined by a basic pleasurable component which has a certain effect on behavior.

Experiences which compromise or qualify a gratification experience for an infant, such as the mother manifesting anxiety or stiffness while providing gratification, are of obvious importance but will not be discussed here. In reality, of course, the various components of the gratification experience are intimately related to one another and have an effect on one another which must be explored for a full understanding of these processes.

During early development, positive reinforcement can be defined in terms of a component of the gratifying actions of the drive object. Most of the time when the infant, in response to an increase in drive tension, behaves in ways that indicate a need for nurturing, he is gratified by the drive object: The mother comes in and holds him or feeds him. The schedule of reinforcement is an almost continuous one. One important implication of such a schedule is its brief extinction time. Behavior influenced by this type of schedule changes easily. After only a few occasions of non-reinforcement, a behavior which in the past elicited reinforcement may become chaotic and then reduce to a low rate and approach zero. In an infant, the baseline or zero functioning would be sporadic drive-determined behavior. In other words, whatever beginning organization had occurred as a consequence of the mother's gratification would be easily lost if her schedule of gratification was a relatively continuous one. This might be explained as over-gratification, which would lead to an inability to tolerate frustration and could be conceptualized as a certain type of, or lack of, full structuralization. For example, some children need continuous external reminders or support if their internal controls or sense of self are to be maintained. If they leave a structured environment or important object, certain ego or superego mechanisms begin to fail. This has been discussed in terms of stimulus nutriment. Rapaport (1958, pp. 19-20), in discussing the interaction of reality with structures, said, "...when such stimulus nutriment is not available, the effectiveness of these structures in controlling id impulses may be impaired and some of the ego's autonomy from the id may be surrendered." The need for stimulus nutriment varies according to the characteristics of the person's structure formation. The concept of the reinforcement schedule provides a framework for partially understanding this aspect of structure formation.

Consider the other extreme—an infant who is gratified in a highly unpredictable manner. Frustrations and gratifications are variable for him. A highly variable schedule with long intervals will lead to a relatively flat extinction curve. Behavior will continue with no reinforcement for long periods of time. Just as the continuous schedule leads to behavior which seems oversensitive to environmental changes, this type of schedule leads to behavior which seems impervious to the environment. Very little stimulus nutriment is necessary to maintain this kind of behavior, which could be conceptualized as overly or prematurely structuralized.

It would be interesting to consider the impact of a variable interval gratification schedule on the child's ability to relinquish developmentally early behavioral patterns for more advanced ones. In order for the child to progress developmentally, early patterns must be at least partially relinquished for new ones. For example, the child must give up patterns involving his symbiotic tie to his mother in order to develop his autonomy and eventually move into a triangular Oedipal configuration. If, however, he is reinforced on a variable interval schedule with particularly long intervals, these early patterns may become so resistant to change that he cannot relinquish them sufficiently to move into more advanced patterns.

At the same time, if patterns which are required for later development are on a continuous schedule, they may be easily lost, and this loss will interfere with later development. For example, certain early organized motor-activity patterns may be essential for the development of differentiated motor skills and the capacity for assertion. If these patterns are reinforced too continuously early in life, they may be vulnerable to regression under conditions of minor frustration.

Many complex schedules of reinforcement have been studied. Most probably the schedules that occur in natural interaction patterns approximate one or another of the established and well-known schedules. If not, an experimental method is available to study the characteristics of those not yet recognized.

Examples of complex schedules are the variable and fixed interval and ratio schedules. A variable ratio schedule has a substantially longer extinction time than does a fixed ratio schedule. A variable interval schedule has a longer extinction time than does a fixed interval schedule. The fixed or variable interval schedule with longer intervals has a longer extinction curve than does its counterpart with shorter intervals. Other schedules, such as concurrent schedules and compound schedules, have their own implications for behavioral change. One theory which has been offered to organize these observations is that the greater the difference between the conditions prevailing during maintenance and during extinction, the quicker will be the extinction, and the more difficult it is to discriminate between the maintenance schedule and the extinction, the slower will be the extinction.

These complex schedules can serve as a framework within which to observe the patterns of gratification that occur in infant rearing. Since each pattern has its own extinction curve with a characteristic time dimension, the pattern of reinforcement may partially determine the stability of the behavioral pattern it influences. Structures which are formed under one kind of gratification pattern will be different in this respect from structures formed under another kind. As the earlier examples illustrate, an infant reinforced for crying on a variable interval schedule with long intervals may stubbornly persist in this behavior even when reinforcement for it ceases and other behaviors are reinforced. On the other hand, an infant reinforced for crying relatively continuously may be able to give up (extinguish) this behavior rather quickly when reinforcement for it ceases and other behaviors are reinforced. The schedule of reinforcement might be looked for as an etiological factor in the genesis of personality organizations which exhibit particular characteristics of change.

Besides variation in the extinction time, the pattern of extinction varies considerably as well, depending on the reinforcement schedule. This may also have implications for structures. The influence of the reinforcement schedule would partially determine how a structure would change in response to a lack of reinforcement. For example, would change occur slowly and evenly, quickly and sporadically, in combinations of these, or how?

For a fixed interval schedule, shortly after the time when reinforcement would have occurred, response ceases abruptly. This is followed by an acceleration of response and another abrupt decline, and so on, until a zero rate of response is approached. This might be seen in an infant who responds to frustration with short bursts of activity or temper. For a variable ratio schedule a high sustained response rate may be emitted during extinction, with longer and longer periods of nonresponse until full extinction is reached. This might be seen in the infant whose temper does not let up in response to frustration until he tires himself out in longer and longer periods of time. A variable interval schedule leads to a slow, steady extinction pattern; this might be seen in the more even-tempered infant. Focusing on these patterns leads to interesting speculations about psychopathological states with different patterns of response to loss which mimic certain of these characteristics, such as depressive, manic, and mixed manic-depressive states. These patterns might be looked for in the etiology of these states.

The reinforcement schedule also determines characteristics of responses while they are being maintained. This process might involve another characteristic of a structure—the way certain structural functions exhibit their actions. For example, different people have different motor patterns, which are influenced by both constitutional factors and the development of the executive substructures of the ego. Under certain schedules, for example, a variable ratio schedule, responses will occur at very high rates, and under others, for example, a variable interval schedule, at very low rates.

Schedules include compound schedules, interlocking schedules, concurrent schedules, and others, each with their own implications for performance during maintenance. Characteristics of temperament and motor activity (e.g., passive versus active children) might in part be determined by the reinforcement schedule.

This discussion has shown that the reinforcement schedule which maintains a function has important implications for that function's stability or resistance to change, its pattern of change, and aspects of its pattern during maintenance.

Thus far the effects of the schedule of reinforcement on the characteristics of structure formation have been discussed in general terms. Oral gratification as a reinforcer for oral behaviors exists at the earliest level of personality organization.

Examining the interaction of environmental stimuli and behavior at this earliest level, where both the response classes and the stimuli which influence them are relatively undifferentiated, does not illustrate fully the use of the model developed in this monograph.

With development and differentiation, the drives and the mental structures which interact with them form new levels of organization. To understand the effect of the reinforcement schedule at these more advanced levels requires a fuller use of the psychoanalytic learning model.

Consider, for example, the phase of development toward the end of the second year of life when the child is beginning to internalize controls. With the beginning establishment of object constancy, he may undertake to discipline himself as his mother has earlier done for him. Later on, with additional internalization, the ego and superego will be formed as complete structures. To observe the effects of the reinforcement schedule at this stage, it is necessary to understand the organization of the child's response and reinforcing stimulus classes.

The child is gaining increased motor ability and control; he is able to internalize the image of another person and to form a relatively constant internal representation; he is able to communicate, using his voice more effectively; he is able to control his sphincter muscles more efficiently. At the same time he is becoming more concerned with approval from his mother and fears the loss of her love, whereas earlier in his development he was more concerned with her presence, whether approving or disapproving. He is also concerned with issues centering on anal-erotic and anal-sadistic tendencies—release, withholding, destruction, smearing, etc. He is developing a capacity for fantasy which will center on some of these issues. These examples suffice to demonstrate how response and stimulus classes are constructed in order to understand the impact of the schedule of reinforcement on structure formation.

Response classes can be constructed on the basis of the new areas of function and concern. For example, the functions pertaining to the internal representation of the mother toward fostering internal control would be one superordinate response class or structure. The functions dealing with motor ability would be another, and the wishes and actions dealing with anal drive derivatives still another. We would have classes or structures dealing with control, motor activity, and drive derivatives.

Stimulus classes could be defined in a similar manner. What is reinforcing to the child at this stage of development will depend on his drive and early ego organization. At this stage he would still be gratified by the earlier oral reinforcers. Some differentiation would already have taken place, however, so that the earlier reinforcers would be modified. During the oral stage almost any contact from the object that reduced frustration or tension was gratifying. But in the anal stage mere object presence or contact may not suffice. Approval, a specific form of contact, is sought. Disapproval by the object may not be experienced as reinforcing. This process will differ among children, of course, but it illustrates the principle of a developing and differentiating drive organization and a parallel development and differentiation of reinforcers.

At this stage partial drives centering on anal-erotic and anal-sadistic trends are also emerging. Their derivatives will define new classes of reinforcers—anal reinforcers. The ego is forming and there is a fear of loss of love which will modify what is experienced as reinforcing. For example, anal-sadistic activities may not be experienced as reinforcing if they are combined with a fear of loss of love. Compromise gratification may evolve in their place.

From the development and differentiation of the oral drives, from the emergence of anal drive derivatives, and from the compromises between the drives and the stage-specific fears, a whole series of new classes of reinforcers will evolve. These, of course, could also be termed structuralized patterns of drive organization. Once these complex organizations of stimuli and responses are identified, it can be observed that the reinforcement schedule affects the formation of structures during this stage, similar to the way it affects structuralization in the oral stage. The reinforcer, the mother's approval, could be presented in different schedules, each with its own implications for resistance to change, pattern while changing, and pattern while functioning, of the response classes or structures of this phase.

It should be mentioned that in this discussion the contingencies of reinforcement are not being examined. The contingency operation defines what behavior will be reinforced and what behavior will not be reinforced. For example, if the mother's approval were contingent on a certain behavior, such as smiling, this behavior or response pattern would increase in frequency. The mother's schedule of approval would then affect certain characteristics of this behavior. In the following discussion and examples the contingency operation will be assumed, and the focus will be on the effects of the schedule of reinforcement.

Consider first the stability or resistance to change of the structure. The stability of the structure dealing with motor control would be directly affected by the mother's schedule of approval. Were the mother's approval on a relatively continuous schedule, motor control would break down if she became unavailable as a reinforcer. If, on the other hand, her schedule of approval was a variable interval one with long intervals, motor control might be quite stable and resistant to change—overcontrolling, perhaps.

The way the control would change owing to a lack of reinforcement would also be affected by the reinforcement schedule. If the motor control functions were on a variable ratio schedule, they might break down from lack of reinforcement in bursts; e.g., there would be erratic episodes of loss of control followed by periods of quiet, etc. If, on the other hand, the schedule were a variable interval one, the loss of control might be slow and steady.

Similarly, the stability or resistance to change and pattern of change of classes of responses centering on anal-sadistic interactions and fantasies would be influenced by the reinforcement schedule affecting them. If these response classes were under the influence of a highly variable schedule, they would be highly resistant to change and would remain an important determinant of later personality organization. But if they were under a fairly continuous schedule of reinforcement, they would change easily, and the responses of the next stage of development might quite easily replace them. In this context the pattern of reinforcement might be looked for as an etiological factor in the genesis of obsessional and hysterical personality organization.

It should not be assumed from this discussion that relatively continuous schedules which provide for relatively little frustration, as compared to that provided by a variable interval or ratio schedule, would necessarily lead to less fixation. The aspect of the gratification experience which can be conceptualized by the schedule of reinforcement is only one component of a process as complex as fixation.

In addition, while patterns under the influence of a continuous schedule tend to change easily and thus to give way to succeeding stages of development, it is well known that certain developmentally early patterns need to be maintained and integrated with later patterns. For example, while it might be useful for a child to relinquish his interest in smearing feces for more phallic interests, it might at the same time be useful for him to retain his interest in regulation. A less continuous or interval schedule might be more likely to lead to the continuation of a pattern that should be retained. In a retrospective analysis, it might be observed that in optimal development different component response patterns of a particular developmental phase are influenced by different schedules of reinforcement. It might also be observed that in maladaptive development the continuation of or lack of establishment of a particular response pattern is related to the maladaptive effects of different schedules of reinforcement. Here again, it should be emphasized that this discussion is about only one dimension of complex processes which involve many interrelated factors.

Another way to use this model would be to follow one area of functioning through its various developmental sequences. For example, consider the responses that deal with self-control and self-punishment. We could follow the superego nuclei through their various stages to full superego formation. At each stage this developing structure could be affected by different reinforcers. We could see if different schedules were associated with different superego characteristics. For example, would a highly variable schedule of reinforcement lead to a rigid superego? Would a highly continuous schedule lead to a superego that constantly needed external support? Would a variable ratio schedule lead to an alternating pattern of superego harshness and permissiveness?

To examine the effect of the reinforcement schedule on the pattern of functioning of a structure, let us consider in a more complex example the different effects of two simple schedules of reinforcement, the variable ratio schedule and the variable interval schedule. The former maintains behaviors at high rates; the latter, at considerably lower rates.

During the oral stage, oral behaviors might come under a variable ratio schedule. As a result of this reinforcement pattern, oral behaviors are frequent. As he enters the anal stage, with the developmental changes considered earlier, particularly the increase in motor activity and the capacity for control, this same schedule remains operative. Now the new response classes are being maintained by the new reinforcers on the variable ratio schedule. The effect of this schedule on the responses under its influence is the same as before: They are emitted at a high rate.

At this stage, therefore, the child, already quite active due to the effect of the variable schedule during infancy, has his activity further augmented by his new motor capacities and by the continuation of the same reinforcement schedule with regard to these new functions.

Yet at this stage another function becomes important: that of self-control resulting from the capacity to internalize the mother's prohibitions, and the mother's continuing reinforcement of this self-controlling function. Her approval appropriately reinforces the child's capacity for self-regulation. This capacity or response class dealing with self-regulation is reinforced on the same variable ratio schedule; it too functions at a high rate. The situation then exists in which two opposing tendencies—structures and response classes—are functioning at a high rate. The child's motor responses are emitted at a high frequency and his attempts at self-control are comparably frequent.

The conflict could result in many different outcomes. One possibility would be that because his activity level and motor responses were established at a high frequency earlier than were the self-controlling responses, they would remain dominant. The result would be a child with a high level of motor activity, who is constantly attempting to curtail it and failing. This process would have profound implications for his self-esteem. Later on he might develop other functions which would mask his frustrated desire to curtail his activity, and he might appear to be a person with an impulse disorder.

This illustration shows how the schedule of reinforcement can affect structural characteristics, that is, the rate at which a function exhibits its action. It demonstrates how, with development and the emergence of new functions, the effects of the reinforcement schedule could become more complex, resulting in conflicts between structures with different tendencies.

To illustrate further, consider what occurs if the variable interval schedule is employed rather than the variable ratio schedule. Like the variable ratio schedule, the variable interval schedule will make the responses it influences resistant to change. But unlike the variable ratio schedule, it will maintain behavior at a low rate.

The child's activity level during the first year of life will be low if it is influenced predominantly by the variable interval schedule, or quite flexible if it is mainly influenced by internal motivations. With increasing motor capacity, assuming the mother employs this schedule, the low rate may prevail or the internal motivation or reinforcement from the activity itself may bring it up to a higher rate.

The maintenance of self-controlling functions under this schedule of the mother's approval will also be at a low rate. The result could be a child with difficulties in self-control or a child who is seemingly relaxed. The variable interval schedule, because it maintains a low rate of response, may not exert as much influence on the child as the higher-rate variable ratio schedule. With the slower rate of response, the child's internal influences may determine his activity level. Of course, if the reinforcement were very infrequent and constitutional tendencies were not reinforced, this type of schedule in its extreme could lead to an apathetic, withdrawn child.

This is a quite different case from the one described in the earlier example. It demonstrates the potential value of analyzing the effects of the reinforcement schedule on the characteristics of a structure.[1] It also demonstrates that understanding the way in which development affects the emergence and organization of new response and stimulus classes makes it possible to study the effects of the schedule of reinforcement on structure formation and functioning throughout development.

The manner in which gratification and frustration are interposed in the life of a child is highly complex. Besides the quality and quantity of gratification, the pattern in which it is experienced may have important implications for the development and character of his mental functions.

B. OTHER LEARNING VARIABLES

Besides the schedule of reinforcement, other learning variables may aid in our better understanding the process of structure formation.

It has been shown how the infant's discriminative capacity influences the broadness of the classes of stimuli and responses. The

---

[1]An interesting speculation arising from consideration of the two schedules considered in the example, the high-rate and the low-rate schedules, is whether there are certain schedules that are optimal for certain infants with particular constitutional styles. It would be interesting to study child-mother interaction patterns, looking at the constitutional style and the pattern of reinforcement, and observe the implications for later development. It would also be interesting to look at the different types of feeding schedules (demand, fixed, etc.) and different methods of toilet training in the context of reinforcement theory. Here too it might be found that different schedules would be optimal for different children.

capacity for the child to make finer and finer discriminations is crucial to the differentiation of these response and stimulus classes. This concept of discriminative capacity and its relationship to the development of classes of responses and stimuli can further our understanding of the relationship between the apparatuses of primary autonomy and structure formation.

If the infant is defective in his perception or processing of stimuli, he will be unable to respond differentially to environmental cues. His early-formed structures will remain broad, general, and undifferentiated. Similarly, precocious maturation of these apparatuses may have implications for premature differentiation. From the side of the environment, the child must receive differential reinforcement or in a more general sense differential responses from his environment for his apparatuses of primary and secondary autonomy to undergo optimal differentiation and lead to structure formation and differentiation. The mother-child relationship which becomes the major vehicle for this differential reinforcement may be studied in terms of an optimal fit where mutual differential reinforcement leads to optimal growth in both parties. Deficiencies or unusual precocities in the discriminative capacity of either party may disrupt this fit. While these are issues that can be discussed without a learning framework, the concepts and experimental data from learning theory can help us focus more precisely on how aspects of discrimination affect specific characteristics of structure formation. For example, the infant who does not discriminate the mother from other adults, either because of a cognitive deficit or a lack of discriminative learning, may indiscriminately associate any object with the nurturing experience. This might lead to later indiscriminate nurturance-seeking behaviors, which would result not only in frustration and disappointment but in faulty relationships.

The concept of the deprivation-satiation operation may help us understand the relationships between the quantity of drive gratification or frustration, and structural differentiation. It was stated earlier that a deprivation operation leads to more behavior related to obtaining the withheld reinforcer. Striving for early reinforcers may often be at the expense of learning behaviors necessary to obtain more advanced ones. Similarly, oversatiation might lead to the infant's inability to develop the complex behavior necessary for gratification in later life. Either situation can lead to a predominance of early structures or action patterns at the expense of differentiation.

7

SUMMARY

Psychoanalytic theory, including the contributions of Hartmann and Erikson, retains the duality of psychological and external reality. Aspects of reality which influence behavior independent of its subjective representations are conceptualized by operant learning theory. This theory focuses on objective properties of external stimuli. In order for psychoanalytic theory to expand its conceptualization of behavior and integrate these learning variables into its framework it must be shown that they can be functionally related to the existing body of theory. To accomplish this, the learning variables are developed in the context of each metapsychological viewpoint. The dynamic point of view identifies the relevant responses and the reinforcing and discriminative stimuli. The genetic point of view defines broad classes of stimuli and responses from a developmental perspective. The economic point of view emphasizes the efficacy or prominence of the stimulus classes, as well as the rigidity of the responses classes. The structural point of view further defines the stimulus and response classes in terms of their broadness, their ingredients, and their relationships with each other. The adaptive point of view demonstrates how classes of stimuli and responses can be defined, not only by drives and structures, but by the interaction of the ego with the environment as well. Each metapsychological perspective contributes to the definition of the learning variables just as each of the analytic perspectives contributes to the definition of the others. The learning variables are therefore distinct concepts which offer a unique view of the multiple determination of behavior and are at the same time capable of sharing with the psychoanalytic perspectives a common framework.

A learning perspective can therefore be formulated in which relationships can be explored between dynamically, genetically, economically, structurally, and adaptively defined behaviors in the present, and similarly defined stimulus configurations which precede and follow them. It was seen how these relationships may influence the final selectiveness of behavior, the frequency of behavior, the modification of behavior, the stability or resistance to change of behavior, and aspects of the configuration and pattern of change of behavior.

When the environmental stimuli are conceptualized as determinants of behavior alongside those recognized by the existing metapsychological points of view, it becomes possible to see in what respect and to what extent the learning variables interact with the other psychoanalytic variables in determining behavior.

The most important implication of the addition of the learning perspective to analytic theory is that it further opens the door of the psychoanalytic discipline to contributions from other behavioral sciences. The learning perspective provides a bridge over which appropriate theoretical and practical aspects of the academic psychologies can travel to be integrated with, and further stimulate, the development of psychoanalysis.

REFERENCES

Akutawaga, D. (1968), Basic Concepts of Anxiety: A Synthesis. *Psychol.*, 5:29-49.

Bandura, A. (1967), Psychotherapy as a Learning Process. In *Sourcebook in Abnormal Psychology*, ed. L. Y. Rabkin & J. E. Carr. Boston: Houghton Mifflin, pp. 474-485.

Birk, L., & Brinkley-Birk, A. W. (1974), Psychoanalysis and Behavior Therapy. *Amer. J. Psychiat.*, 131:499-510.

Blom, G. E. (1972), A Psychoanalytic Viewpoint of Behavior Modification in Clinical and Educational Settings. *J. Amer. Acad. Child Psychiat.*, 11:675-694.

Brady, J. P. (1967), Psychotherapy, Learning Theory, and Insight. *Arch. Gen. Psychiat.*, 16:304-311.

Cahoon, D. D. (1968), Symptom Substitution and the Behavior Therapies: A Reappraisal. *Psychol. Bull.*, 69:149-156.

Dollard, J., & Miller, N. E. (1950), *Personality and Psychotherapy.* New York: McGraw-Hill.

Erikson, E. H. (1956), The Problem of Ego Identity. *J. Amer. Psychoanal. Assn.*, 4:56-121.

Escalona, S. (1963), Patterns of Infantile Experience. *The Psychoanalytic Study of the Child,* 18:197-244. New York: International Universities Press.

Feather, B. W., & Rhoads, J. M. (1972), Psychodynamic Behavior Therapy. *Arch. Gen. Psychiat.*, 26:496-511.

Ferster, C. B., & Skinner, B. F. (1957), *Schedules of Reinforcement.* New York: Appleton-Century-Crofts.

Freud, S. (1894), The Neuro-Psychoses of Defence. *Standard Edition,* 3:45-61. London: Hogarth Press, 1962.

——— (1900), The Interpretation of Dreams. *Standard Edition,* 4 & 5. London: Hogarth Press, 1953.

——— (1911), Formulations on the Two Principles of Mental Functioning. *Standard Edition,* 12:218-226. London: Hogarth Press, 1958.

——— (1923), The Ego and the Id. *Standard Edition,* 19:12-66. London: Hogarth Press, 1961.

Gewirtz, J. L. (1969), Some Contextual Determinants of Stimulus Potency. Paper presented at the meeting of the Society for Research in Child Development, March 26.

Goldiamond, I. (1968), Some Applications and Implications of Behavioral Analysis for Psychotherapy. *Research in Psychotherapy* (American Psychological Association), 3:54-89.

Hartmann, H. (1939), *Ego Psychology and the Problem of Adaptation.* New York: International Universities Press, 1958.

———, Kris, E., & Loewenstein, R. M. (1946), The Formation of Psychic Structure. In Papers on Psychoanalytic Psychology. *Psychol. Issues,* Monogr. 14:27-55. New York: International Universities Press, 1964.

Holt, R. R. (1967), Ego Autonomy Re-evaluated. *Internat. J. Psychiat.,* 3:481-503.

Hunt, H. F., & Dyrud, V. F. (1968), Commentary—Perspective in Behavior Therapy. *Research in Psychotherapy* (American Psychological Association), 3:140-152.

Lewin, K. (1926), Intention, Will, and Need. In *Organization and Pathology of Thought,* ed. D. Rapaport. New York: Columbia University Press, 1951, pp. 95-153.

Mahler, M. (1963), Thoughts about Development and Individuation. *The Psychoanalytic Study of the Child,* 18:307-324. New York: International Universities Press.

Marks, I. M., & Gelder, M. G. (1966), Common Ground between Behavior Therapy and Psychodynamic Methods. *Brit. J. Med. Psychol.,* 39:11-23.

Marmor, J. (1969), Neurosis and the Psychotherapeutic Process: Similarities and Differences in the Behavioral and Psychodynamic Conceptions. *Internat. J Psychiat.,* 7:514-519.

——— (1971), Dynamic Psychotherapy and Behavior Therapy. *Arch. Gen. Psychiat.,* 24:22-29.

Miller, N. E. (1964), Some Implications of Modern Behavior Therapy for Personality Change and Psychotherapy. In *Personality Change,* ed. P. Worchel & D. Byrne. New York: Wiley, pp. 149-175.

——— (1969), Visceral Learning and Other Additional Facts Potentially Applicable to Psychotherapy. *Internat. Psychiat. Clin.,* 6:294-312.

Mowrer, O. H. (1950), *Learning Theory and Personality Dynamics.* New York: Ronald Press.

Rapaport, D. (1958), The Theory of Ego Autonomy: A Generalization. *Bull. Menninger Clin.,* 22:13-35.

——— (1959), The Structure of Psychoanalytic Theory: A Systematizing Attempt. *Psychol. Issues,* Monogr. 6. New York: International Universities Press, 1960.

Reynolds, G. S. (1968), *A Primer of Operant Conditioning.* Glenview, Ill.: Scott Foresman.

Ritvo, S., & Solnit, A. (1958), Influence of the Early Mother-Child Interaction on the Identification Processes. *The Psychoanalytic Study of the Child,* 13:64-91. New York: International Universities Press.

Skinner, B. F. (1938), *The Behavior of Organisms.* New York: Appleton-Century-Crofts.

Weiner, H. (1964), Conditioning History and Human Fixed Interval Performances. *J. Exp. Anal. Behav.,* 7:383-385.

——— (1965), Conditioning History and Maladaptive Human Operant Behavior. *Psychol. Rep.,* 17:935-942.

Weitzman, B. (1967), Behavior Therapy and Psychotherapy. *Psychol. Rev.,* 74:300-317.

Wolf, E. (1969), Learning Theory and Psychoanalysis. *Internat. J. Psychiat.,*

    7:525-535.

Wolff, P. H. (1960), The Developmental Psychologies of Jean Piaget and Psychoanalysis. *Psychol. Issues,* Monogr. 5. New York: International Universities Press.

Woody, R. H. (1968), Toward a Rationale for Psychobehavioral Therapy. *Arch. Gen. Psychiat.,* 19:197-204.

INDEX

ABOUT THE AUTHOR

STANLEY I. GREENSPAN received his M.D. from Yale University School of Medicine in 1966. He received training in adult psychiatry at Columbia Presbyterian Medical Center, New York City, in child psychiatry at Hillcrest Children's Center, Children's Hospital, Washington, D. C., and in 1970 became a research psychiatrist at the Laboratory of Psychology, National Institute of Mental Health. He is now Deputy Director and Director of Clinical Research at the Mental Health Study Center of the National Institute of Mental Health.